KW-467-320

This book is to be returned on
or before the date stamped below

POLYTECHNIC SOUTH WEST

ACADEMIC SERVICES
Plymouth Library
Tel: (0752) 232323
This book is subject to recall if required by another reader
Books may be renewed by phone
CHARGES WILL BE MADE FOR OVERDUE BOOKS

The Shadow Economy in Britain and Germany

THE SHADOW ECONOMY IN BRITAIN AND GERMANY

Based on a comparative research project undertaken by the Institute for Fiscal Studies, London, and the *Institut für Angewandte Wirtschaftsforschung, Tübingen.*

Stephen Smith and Susanne Wied-Nebbeling

a project of the
ANGLO-GERMAN FOUNDATION
FOR THE STUDY OF INDUSTRIAL SOCIETY

The Anglo-German Foundation for the Study of Industrial Society was established by an agreement between the British and German governments after a state visit to Britain by the late President Heinemann, and incorporated by Royal Charter in 1973. Funds were initially provided by the German government; since 1979, both governments have been contributing.

The Foundation aims to contribute to the knowledge and understanding of industrial society in the two countries and to promote contacts between them. It funds selected research projects and conferences on industrial, economic, and social subjects designed to be of practical use to policymakers.

Printed by George Over Ltd, London and Rugby

Anglo-German Foundation for the Study of Industrial Society
17 Bloomsbury Square, London, WC1A 2LP

Contents

Preface

This study is based on the results of a comparative research project on the shadow economy in Britain and West Germany, undertaken jointly by the *Institut für Angewandte Wirtschaftsforschung* and the Institute for Fiscal Studies, and funded by the Anglo-German Foundation.

Much of the detail of the results for Britain and West Germany has been written up in separate country reports (Petry and Wied-Nebbeling, 1986, for West Germany, and Smith, 1986, for Britain). In this study we aim to highlight the comparative aspects of the research, and in particular to consider what can be learned from a comparison of the experiences of the two countries.

We are grateful for the assistance we have received during the course of this project from many individuals and organisations. In particular, colleagues at the two institutes have been involved at various stages of the research. At IAW, the report on the shadow economy in Germany was written jointly by Günther Petry and Susanne Wied-Nebbeling, whilst at IFS the initial stages of the project were undertaken by Nick Morris. Michael Kell, Chris Pissarides and Guglielmo Weber were also closely involved in various aspects of the IFS research.

We wish to record our appreciation of the assistance of the Anglo-German Foundation in establishing the collaboration between the two institutes, and in financial support for the research. Barbara Beck and Hans Wiener, Secretary General and Projects Director respectively of the Foundation, have taken an active interest in the research, and we are grateful for their advice and encouragement. Amanda Claremont has capably handled the preparation of this report for publication within a very tight time-table.

Responsibility for the views expressed in this report, and for any errors that remain, rests with the authors alone.

1 Introduction

The last few years have been boom years for academic papers on the shadow economy. The flood of research began with a paper by Gutmann in 1977, in which he estimated that the US shadow economy in the previous year had amounted to 10 per cent of official Gross National Product. Other papers followed. In very little time an almost unmanageable variety of concepts, definitions and measurement attempts had appeared. Estimates of its size varied widely. Some of the estimates which attracted the greatest publicity suggested that the shadow economy had grown sharply in importance, and now comprised a substantial proportion of all productive activity in the economy.

The academic interest in the shadow economy has gone hand in hand with growing public concern in both Britain and Germany about the effects of the shadow economy; some of the larger estimates of its importance may indeed have fuelled this concern in no small measure. At a time when unemployment in both countries was rising to levels unprecedented in the post-war period, the possibility of job losses in the legitimate economy as a result of illegal competition from 'moonlighters' and *Schwarzarbeiter* took on far greater urgency. In addition, as public expenditure — especially expenditure on social insurance benefits — came under increasing pressure in both countries, and concern began to be expressed about the level of taxation, people began to pay greater attention to the possibility that both public expenditure and taxes were much higher than they would need to be if tax evasion and the abuse of social security benefits could be controlled.

Thirdly, the long post-war boom had come to an end; the rate of growth of GDP had fallen, and the reasons for this were the subject of much anguished debate. It was hardly surprising that considerable interest would be aroused by claims that these problems were all an 'illusion' — that levels of production and employment and the rate of growth had been systematically under-estimated because official statisticians ignored the shadow economy, and failed to take into account the growing amounts of production by moonlighters, or through do-it-yourself work, voluntary organisations, etc. These, it was argued, were the boom areas of the seventies and eighties; but were areas which conventional thinking still failed to acknowledge, and official policy largely ignored.

Both in Britain and in Germany these ideas have gained in currency. Some, indeed, such as the belief that the level of tax evasion has been rising, have become almost conventional wisdom. But much of the discussion in Britain and Germany has been very parochial. Despite this, it is clear that many of the issues under discussion are the same, and that there is similar uncertainty about the causes, the size, and the consequences of the shadow economy. In this study we take a comparative view, with the aim of seeing what light the experiences of two similar countries — but nevertheless countries which differ in a number of important institutional respects — might shed on the scale of the shadow economy, and on policy issues.

Definitions

In this study we attach a broad meaning to the concept of the shadow economy. By the shadow economy we mean all productive activity which does not take place in the formal economy. The shadow economy includes the non-market productive activities of households and voluntary organisations (which we might refer to as the 'self-service economy' or the 'non-profit economy'). It also includes market-economy transactions which are purposely concealed from the authorities, either because they are illegal, or to facilitate the evasion of taxes and social insurance contributions (frequently called the 'black economy').

Figure 1.1 shows an overview of the terms we use in this report, and indicates how the shadow economy and formal economy are related. Figure 1.2 gives a range of examples of the activities which we include in each part of the shadow economy, and may help the reader to give content to the above definitions.

One aspect of shadow economy activities is that they are frequently less subject to government regulation than activities in the formal economy, either because they are hidden from the eyes of the state (black economy) or because, in most countries, productive activities within the family have usually been regarded as outside the legitimate range of government authority. Exceptions can be found: for example, the licensing system for home brewing in existence in the UK up until the 1960s. But whilst the lack of government regulation may not be a defining characteristic of the shadow economy, it is clearly an important aspect of many shadow economy activities.

One aspect of government involvement in particular, the extent of taxation, is an important contrast between the shadow and formal economies. Both the black economy, where many activities are hidden to avoid tax and social insurance contributions, and the household economy and voluntary sector, whose productive activities are rarely subject to tax, are sectors where, by and large, productive activity can take place without taxes being levied. In contrast, in the formal sector, most productive activity is subject to tax. The absence of taxation on activities in the shadow economy links a wide range of otherwise rather unrelated activities, and provides a common framework for much analysis of the shadow economy. We will return at a number of places in this report to the question of whether taxation has encouraged the substitution of activity in the shadow economy for equivalent productive activity in the formal economy.

A number of important points about the above definition of the shadow economy deserve emphasis. The first is that it should be clear that we are talking about an 'economy'; in other words about an area of **economic activity**. When we refer to the 'size' of the shadow economy, what we mean is the amount of **value added** created by shadow economy activities. In the case of the voluntary/household economy this is perhaps clear enough, but there has often been confusion about what is meant by the size of the black economy.

Figure 1.1   Defining the Shadow Economy

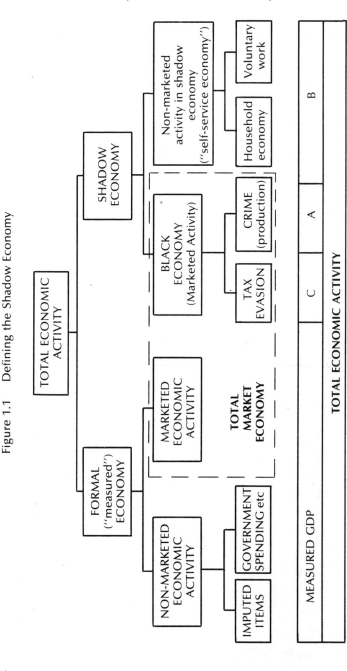

A — activities which should, in principle, be measured in GDP, but are not because they are hidden
B — activities excluded from GDP by convention
C — shadow economy activities included in GDP

Figure 1.2   Examples of shadow economy activities

SHADOW ECONOMY	
BLACK ECONOMY	**SELF-SERVICE ECONOMY**
* Moonlighting (after-hours work conducted on a private basis, with earnings not declared for tax)	* Housework (cooking, cleaning, etc)
* Other tax evasion by second-job holders	* DIY home repairs and decoration
* Tax evasion by the self-employed (eg by "off-the-books" business, charging private purchases as company expenses, etc)	* Gardening, sewing, dressmaking
* Undeclared rental incomes	* Childcare, care of aged relatives
* Undeclared interest, dividends, etc	* Private transport
* "Working and claiming" by the unemployed	* Voluntary work for charities, political parties, churches, etc
* Drug trafficking and other illegal businesses	* Informal voluntary help to neighbours, friends and relatives
	* Administration of clubs and societies

The amount of value added in the black economy (or, equivalently, the level of concealed factor income) is not necessarily the same as the amount of income on which tax is evaded (nor yet the amount of tax that the government fails to collect because of evasion). Taxable incomes may include transfer payments — such as interest on government debt — in addition to factor incomes. Whilst such transfer payments may be subject to tax, and may therefore also be subject to tax evasion, they do not reflect any addition to Gross Domestic Product, but merely redistribute it. The total extent of income on which tax is evaded may, for some purposes, be an interesting question, but our main focus in this report is instead on the amount of economic activity which is concealed in order to evade taxes and social insurance contributions. For this purpose the concepts of economic income and value added are clearly appropriate.

The second feature of our definition of the shadow economy is that the scope of the shadow economy may differ from country to country. Certain activities may count as part of the formal economy in one country, but fall into the shadow economy in another. There are two principal reasons why this may be so.

Firstly, there are reasons connected with the legal and taxation framework. One country may tax a wider range of activities than another, and, as a result, a wider range of activities may be concealed to evade these taxes. Between Britain and Germany there are some differences in the goods subject to VAT, with food being zero-rated in the UK, for example. But the tax threshold for income tax is broadly the same in the two countries. Similarly, some activities may be illegal in one country but not in another. As Blades (1982) has noted, the value added in hidden criminal activities in the USA is likely to be greater than in most other OECD countries because a wider range of activities are illegal in the USA than elsewhere. Between Britain and Germany there are also differences, for example in the kinds of gambling and card games permitted and forbidden, and in the legal status of prostitution.

A second reason for the differences in scope of the definition between countries is that patterns of behaviour may differ. Certain activities which generally take place in the formal economy in one country may take place in the shadow economy in another. This may be particularly true of comparisons between developed and less-developed countries. In less-developed countries a range of activities may frequently take place within the household economy, which in more industrialised economies are commonly the subject of market transactions. It is for this reason that the GDP produced in the formal economy alone is regarded as a poor indicator of the difference in living standards between countries at different stages of development, and that the extension of such comparisons to include economic activity in the shadow economy has been advocated. Between countries which are at a similar level of development, such as the UK and Germany, such differences in scope may well be less. But they may nonetheless exist. In the UK, for example, most new houses are built by big companies for subsequent sale, whilst in Germany it is quite common for individuals to be involved in the building of their own houses, and on occasion to supply their own labour. A part of new house building may thus take place in the shadow economy in Germany, but to a much lesser extent in the UK.

The National Accounts and the Shadow Economy

Economic activity in the shadow economy may not be reflected in the national accounts for one of two broad reasons. Firstly some productive activities, such as housework, which are included in the shadow economy fall outside the definition of 'economic activity' used in the national accounts. Most of the value added in the self-service economy is in fact excluded from the national accounts for this reason. Secondly, other activities which in principle ought to be included in the national accounts may be missed out, or simply guessed because of a lack of information about their extent. Examples of this could be incomes on which tax was being evaded, and which were therefore not reported to the authorities, and factor incomes from some criminal activities such as prostitution and the drug trade. Nevertheless, as we shall show, not all of the value added in the black economy is omitted from the national accounts: because of the way the accounts are compiled, some of the value added in the black economy is in fact reflected in the estimates of GDP.

Principles of the National Accounts
The national accounts measure the money value of goods and services becoming available to the nation from economic activity — or equivalently, the incomes which are derived from economic activity. The incomes that count are the incomes of factors of production, or 'factor incomes'. Transfer payments for which no goods or services are received in return, such as pensions, social security and gifts, do not increase the national income total. This is because they do not increase the total spending power of the economy, but merely transfer spending power from one person to another.

The Shadow Economy in Britain and Germany

In both Britain and Germany, the National Accounts focus mainly on market transactions. The German *Statistisches Bundesamt* observes that 'Market transactions stand at the centre of economic observations in a market economy, portrayal is based first and foremost on coverage of market transactions'. (*Statistiches Bundesamt*, 1982, p67, our translation). The UK Central Statistical Office takes the same view:

> 'In computing a money measure of the nation's production, it is most convenient to confine attention to activities yielding goods and services which can be given a value which is not wholly arbitrary. This means substantially those goods and services which are in fact exchanged for money'. (Maurice, 1968, p7)

In fact two types of economic activity are included in both countries' National Accounts. Economic activity associated with the production and sale of marketed goods and services forms the greater part of GDP; the goods and services involved can be valued straightforwardly at the prices at which they are transacted in the market place. The production of goods and services by the state is also included in GDP. Whilst the output of national defence and other government services is not normally traded, the inputs used — labour, materials and so on — do have a market value, and it is this value which is used as the basis for estimating the value of the output of the government sector. Most household production, by contrast, involves neither traded outputs nor, completely, traded inputs, and is largely omitted from the national accounts of both countries.

In practice, in neither country is the boundary of the national accounts drawn precisely at this point. In both countries the national accounts statistics extend a little beyond marketed production and the government sector to cover certain further kinds of economic activity which are not the subject of monetary transactions. This is done in order 'not to leave out of account significant parts of non-market economic activity which are of significance in the observation and analysis of economic events'. (*Statistiches Bundesamt* 1982, p7, our translation).

The argument is that there are certain parts of the economy where substitution between the formal economy and the shadow economy may be so great that Gross Domestic Product might prove an inadequate indicator of changes in total economic activity over time, or of the differences in living standards between countries. Thus, for example, it is pointed out that a shift in the pattern of housing tenure from rental to owner-occupation might appear to lead to a fall in Gross Domestic Product, unless an amount were imputed in the national accounts for the own rental incomes notionally earned by owner-occupiers. Similarly, comparisons of GDP between countries with a different balance of owner-occupied and rented property would be misleading unless rental income were imputed to owner-occupiers.

In both the UK and Germany the national accounts do indeed include an imputed rental income on owner-occupied housing. Other non-market transactions for which a valuation is made in the national accounts are in quantitative terms quite important, and are generally confined to cases where a 'reasonably satisfactory basis for the assumed valuation is available' (Maurice, 1968, p8). Usually these cases are those where the imputed transactions can be valued by comparison with other transactions where money changes hands. Both in the British and the German national accounts, values are imputed for a number of incomes-in-kind, such as the meals that restaurant workers and seamen receive, the free coal received by coal miners, the private use of company cars, etc. In the UK accounts these adjustments amount in total to less than one per cent of total wages and salaries. Apart from this, non-market shadow economy activities are largely omitted from the UK national acounts.

In Germany the principal difference in the treatment of shadow economy activities in the national accounts is the inclusion of an estimated value for the work which private households themselves do in the construction of houses and other dwellings. As we have already noted, it seems to be a more common occurrence in Germany than in Britain for people to be actively involved in the construction of their own new homes, and the labour supplied in this way is believed to be a not insignificant contribution to the aggregate value of new house-building. Petry and Wied-Nebbeling (1986) describe the way in which the *Statistiches Bundesamt* makes its assessment of the value of both own-labour and moonlighters' labour involved in housing construction. Essentially, the labour hours contributed through the shadow economy are valued on the basis of the building materials used, using the cost structure of similar activities in the formal economy.

Whilst there are thus some minor differences in the coverage, in principle, of the National Accounts in the UK and Germany, they are not in quantitative terms of any real importance. Of perhaps more interest are the differences in the way in which concealed economic activities in the black economy may affect the accuracy of the national accounts in each country.

Concealed Transactions

What we have, in this report, referred to as the 'black economy' causes special problems for national accounts statisticians. Most of the hidden economic activity in the black economy should, in principle, be included in the national accounts. For example, off-the-books business on which VAT is evaded, or moonlighting work for cash, are both areas of market economy activity which, according to the principles outlined above, should be included in the national accounts. (Arguably, an exception might be made for black economy activities which are in themselves illegal, such as the production and sale of illegal drugs). The problem is that what has been hidden from the eyes of the taxman may also be obscured from the view of the national accounts statisticians, and therefore may not be reflected properly in the national accounts.

The extent to which the national accounts fail to pick up black economy transactions depends fundamentally on the way in which the accounts are compiled. Different statistical sources will be differently affected by the problem of concealed incomes. In this there are major differences between the national accounts of Britain and Germany. The UK national accounts compiled from the income side are largely based on the amounts of income that individual taxpayers declare for tax, and are thus believed to be significantly affected by the omission of the tax evaders' incomes. On the expenditure side the estimates are based on survey data which is believed to be less affected by the black economy. The difference between the two, indeed, is used to make an estimate of the extent to which the income measure of GDP has been underestimated due to tax evasion. Ultimately, reliance is placed on the expenditure data to determine the level of GDP. The income data are in effect used merely to determine the division of factor incomes on the income side of the accounts, and the fact that the income data are affected by evasion should not introduce errors into the estimates of the level of GDP. On the other hand, were the black economy to lead to errors in the expenditure data, this could affect the GDP estimates. (This point is discussed further in Chapter 5.)

The estimates of GDP and GNP in the German national accounts are, by contrast, based primarily on the output (or 'income creation') estimates, which are based on production statistics. The distribution of factor incomes is calculated using income statistics and tax statistics, and the expenditure side of the accounts is based on statistics of foreign trade, investment and finance. All three sides of the accounts are harmonised before the figures are published, and the published data therefore do not give any scope for estimating the extent of concealed incomes. Nevertheless, whilst little information is published about how the *Statistisches Bundesamt* makes its calculations, it is clear that any shortfall in the income estimate of GDP below the output estimate will have been corrected — implicitly or explicitly — by the addition of an amount reflecting incomes concealed from taxation. Thus, as in the UK, concealment of income is unlikely in itself to affect the accuracy of the GDP estimates. Only if the black economy in Germany leads to understatement of the level of production is GDP likely to be underestimated. Ultimately, therefore, whether the black economy affects the estimates of the level of GDP will depend on the accuracy of the production statistics in Germany, but on the accuracy of expenditure statistics in the UK.

2 Reasons for activities in the shadow economy

Much of our interest in the shadow economy concerns areas where substitution may take place between activities in the formal economy and activities in the shadow economy. It is at these points where changes may be occurring that should be taken account of in our perception of economic events. It is also in these areas of substitutability where public policy decisions are most likely to influence the development of the shadow economy, and the division of activities between the formal and shadow economies.

Gershuny and Pahl (1979) and Cassell (1982) have illustrated some of these substitutions with the aid of the triangular diagram shown in Figure 2.1. This shows the two main components of the shadow economy, the underground or black economy, and the 'self-service' economy, comprising both the household economy and the activities of voluntary organisations. Substitution may transfer economic activities between each of these two parts of the shadow economy and the formal economy, or indeed, between the self-service economy and the underground economy.

The substitutions marked 1 in the figure involve the transfer of activities between the self-service economy and the formal economy. It is commonly held that the process of industrialisation has involved the gradual 'formalisation' of economic activity previously taking place within the self-service economy. Thus, for example,

Figure 2.1   Substitutions between the formal economy and the shadow economy

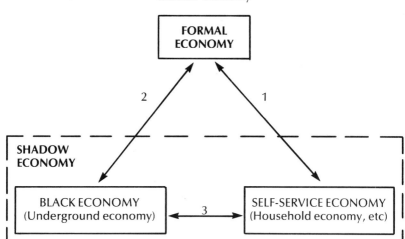

there has been an increasing tendency over time for people to buy clothes rather than to make them, to buy convenience foods rather than to prepare meals, and so on. Latterly, both the upbringing of children and the care of the sick and elderly have both begun to move over into the formal economy, through the growth of kindergartens, hospitals, old people's homes, etc. But there have also been substitutions in the other direction, such as the growth of 'do-it-yourself' and an increasing tendency for self-service in some other areas. Gershuny (1983) has argued that in the post-war period many services which relatively wealthy households had formerly purchased through the formal economy, by employing cooks, home helps, etc, began instead to be provided by a mixture of household capital goods (food processors, dishwashers, vacuum cleaners etc) and self-service labour.

The substitutions marked 2 in Figure 2.1 involve the margin of substitution between the formal economy and the black economy. A growing amount of moonlighting and other activities evading sales and income taxes would represent substitution away from the formal economy. On the other hand, increasing firm size, greater enforcement efforts or technical changes in payment and accounting mechanisms might encourage substitutions back in the other direction, towards the formal economy.

The substitutions marked 3, taking place within the shadow economy, between the black economy and the self-service economy, are perhaps of less interest in the present context. What is of decisive importance in determining the size of the shadow economy, and its evolution over time, is the overall balance of positive and negative substitutions between the formal and shadow economies — in other words, the overall impact of the substitutions marked 1 and 2. In this chapter we aim to identify some of the factors which may affect these processes of substitution, and hence determine the balance between the formal and shadow economies.

Some writers have approached this question at a very general level, and have sought to identify the causes underlying the shadow economy as a whole. Tuchtfeldt (1984, p24ff), for example, identifies the following reasons for the existence of the shadow economy:-

- growth of the burden of taxation
- growth of National Insurance contributions
- a growing burden of regulations
- growth of other cost pressures
- increase in the percentage of foreign residents
- reduction in working hours
- reduction in the acceptance of state authority.

Other writers have added to this list. Frey and Pommerehne (1983 pp280ff) have pointed to the role that the conjunctural situation in the labour market may play in encouraging the supply of labour to the shadow economy, and Buttler (1983, pp20ff) has observed that people may be attracted to the shadow economy because it may at times provide considerably more job satisfaction than work in the formal economy.

This general approach to the causes of economic activity in the shadow economy does have the merit of highlighting some factors, such as the growth in taxation in the formal economy, reductions in working hours, and so on, which may have similar effects across a wide range of shadow economy activities. On the other hand, analysis at this level fails to take account of the heterogeneity of the various activities included within the shadow economy. At the very least, the weighting or relative importance of the different causes listed above will differ for different parts of the shadow economy. It is possible also that other factors too may have exerted an influence on the development of certain individual parts of the shadow economy. The following discussion of the causes of the shadow

economy reflects the variety of activities, and of causes, by considering separately the major parts of the shadow economy.

Reasons for economic activity in the household economy

The household economy is no new phenomenon. Indeed, from a
historical point of view, it was the starting-point for economic
activity. Many activities such as cooking, cleaning, childcare and so
on have in most households always been part of the household
economy. In looking for 'causes' of economic activity in the household economy we are looking for reasons why such activities have
almost exclusively been within the household economy rather than
the formal economy, and for the characteristics of activities where a
greater tendency for substitution between the formal and household economies exists. We may consider separately a number of
activities within the household economy.

Housework and gardening
This area has tended to be determined most strongly by tradition
and social conventions; in particular, housework such as cleaning,
washing up and washing clothes, and also gardening, appear to be
largely independent of many of the causes for shadow economy
activities listed earlier (taxation, the burden of government regulations, etc). An alternative to provision within the household is rarely
sought, not only because of the cost of market alternatives, but
because housework is done as a matter of course by most housewives (though by fewer husbands ...). Housework thus forms a fairly
stable core of economic activity within the household economy.

That is not to say that there are no areas of possible substitution
between the household economy and the formal economy. Whilst
few households now employ cooks, a considerable number of
households still employ home helps, and over the post-war period
there has in fact been a considerable change in the way in which
such work has been done in certain kinds of household, within the
UK at least. Gershuny (1983) has argued that quite a sharp rise took
place between the 1930s and the 1960s in the amount of time that
middle-class housewives in the UK spent on housework, probably
reflecting a fall in the number of paid servants.

Changes have also taken place in the 'technologies' available for housework. Washing clothes has been made easier not only through the development of washing machines and spin dryers, but also through the development of other new products such as drip-dry clothes, disposable nappies, etc. The use of laundries, and probably also the employment of domestic labour to wash clothes, has declined as these improvements have made the task of self-service easier. Similarly, the development of convenience foods, and the widespread use of new techniques such as freezing and microwave cookery have both reduced the amount of labour time required for household production and increased the range of formal economy/household economy substitution options which are available.

Transport, shopping
Over the past few decades there have been dramatic changes in the way that these activities are performed. Widespread car ownership has increased the scope for self-provision of transport services and has indeed opened up a wide range of travel opportunities for most households. A purely economic calculation, whilst it may lie in the background, is rarely a decisive influence on the choice of private rather than public transport. Surveys of the reasons for car ownership have tended to give prominence to factors such as convenience and comfort, rather than cost factors.

Shopping too, has undergone a revolution in recent years, with the spread of self-service shops and supermarkets, and, increasingly, the introduction of automation through bank cash machines, automatic ticket machines and petrol stations. Economic factors clearly have had an influence here, and the lower costs of self-service stores, passed on in lower prices, have been an important aspect of the process of competition. They may not have been the only factor; customer preference for self-service shopping, automatic cash dispensers, etc may have played a part too. The extra labour time may not in fact be all that important: the customer has to be present whilst shopping both in self-service shops and in shops where a more personal service is given. In this respect shopping and transport are rather similar; the move to self-service shopping, like the switch to self-provision of transport services, may involve greater individual effort, but no greater expenditure of time.

Caring activities

A recent development has been the reduction in the extent to which the care of children, the sick and the old has taken place within the household. Old people's homes, hospitals, kindergartens and play-groups have contributed to a growing formal economy alternative to care within the household economy. The reasons for this are complex. In particular, the growing participation of women within the formal economy — perhaps in itself related to declining family size, but also quite clearly to cultural and social factors — may have contributed to (or been a reflection of?) the increasing formalisation of caring. But it is clear that this is an area where social attitudes and pressures play a major role, and it would be implausible to suggest that economic factors have been major determinants of the changes that have taken place.

Production of other goods and services

An appreciable expansion in do-it-yourself activities within the household economy appears to have taken place during the 1970s. Pahl (1984, p101) reckons that between 1974 and 1980 consumer spending on DIY goods, tools and home decorating in the UK grew by 19 per cent in real terms, compared to 8 per cent for all consumer spending. In Germany over the same period spending on tools for DIY work doubled, but spending on the materials for home decoration grew more slowly than total private consumption. One factor amongst this DIY boom, according to Pahl, has been the expansion of home ownership; home owners typically spend much more on DIY than tenants. Other factors may have been increasing free time (both as a result of rising unemployment and of reductions in working hours), the pleasure that may be derived from DIY, and the rising cost of employing labour in the formal economy. A significant percentage of DIY enthusiasts may actually be able to do the job better themselves than by hiring a handyman in the formal economy, who may be less motivated to do a good job. The development of new materials and products too, has 'de-skilled' many DIY jobs, increasing the ability of untrained householders to obtain satisfactory results from their own DIY efforts.

For many areas, then, of household production, economic causes would appear to play only a limited role. Tradition and social pressures exert a much greater influence, and constrain — at least in the short term — the amount of substitution that may take place between the formal and household sectors. Economic factors, including both wage rates and levels of taxation may, however, form part of the backdrop against which longer term social changes affect the division of labour between the formal economy and household production. Over time, attitudes may change under the influence of economic pressures, and technological developments (the vacuum cleaner, automatic bank tellers, 'Polyfilla') may also arise, in part at least, in response to the changing cost of formal economy alternatives.

Reasons for economic activity in voluntary organisations

The range of voluntary organisations is extremely wide, and the range of motivations correspondingly diverse. A distinction might however, be drawn between voluntary organisations based on 'reciprocity' and those based on 'altruism'. By reciprocity in this context we mean that those who work in the organisation expect to benefit themselves from the services it provides. Examples of 'reciprocal' voluntary organisations include football clubs, baby-sitting circles, housing co-operatives and local amenity groups. Voluntary organisations based on altruism are those where the people supplying the work effort are different people to those who are likely to benefit from the activities of the organisation. Charities providing assistance to the sick and the needy are the clearest examples of 'altruistic' voluntary bodies.

The borderline between the two concepts is difficult to define in practice, and the motivation of people who supply labour to voluntary organisations has been vigorously disputed (see Gerard, 1983). Without wishing to impugn the motives of those who devote their free time to voluntary work it may be observed that quite a wide range of activities can plausibly be seen as having an element of reciprocity. Whilst the organisers of a youth club, for example, may be well above the age to benefit themselves from its activities, they may hope that their children will one day benefit. Even if they have no children themselves, they may hope that their work will contribute to a sense of 'community', and the maintenance of a range of communal activities from some of which they may indeed benefit.

Whilst voluntary organisations of both types may be seen as responding to the absence (or inadequate provision) of formal economy alternatives, the activities of charities and other 'altruistic' organisations are likely to be less sensitive to the terms on which formal economy alternatives are available. Economic motivations are unlikely to play much part in the willingness of people to work in 'altruistic' organisations, still less in the responses of the disadvantaged people they help. A case can be made, however, for a greater role for the influence of economic factors in the activities of some purely reciprocal voluntary organisations: baby-sitting circles, for example, are more likely to be organised if the cost of employing a baby-sitter is high than if baby-sitters can be employed cheaply and easily. Similarly, co-operative labour supply in housebuilding — a phenomenon more common in Germany than in Britain — is largely a response to the high cost of formal economy labour. On the other hand, some aspects of reciprocal voluntary organisations do not directly substitute for services available in the formal economy. Tennis clubs, for example, may perform various social functions and provide social status for those holding positions of reponsibility in them, for which there is no direct counterpart in the tennis facilities provided through the formal economy.

Reasons for the black economy

The black economy is, in contrast to the household/voluntary economy, a market economy. As a result, economic factors are perhaps more likely to play a significant role in determining the level of activity in this part of the shadow economy, and in the process of substitution between the formal and shadow economies. Amongst economic factors, the levels of taxation and social insurance contributions are perhaps the most frequently cited possible causes both for the alleged growth of tax evasion by existing producers of goods and services, and the development of alternatives to the formal economy such as moonlighting.

Economists' theoretical models of tax evasion have generally regarded the individual's decision whether to try to evade tax as being based on a rational profit-maximising calculation. These models are well surveyed by Cowell (1985). Tax evasion, in this view, has potential benefits and potential costs to the individual concerned. The principal benefit if the evasion is successful is the saving of tax that would otherwise have to be paid. The potential cost, however, against which the benefit has to be weighed, is the risk of being caught, and the penalties, including the possibility of fines and a criminal record, that could follow. The higher the potential benefits in relation to the costs and risk of detection, the more likely an individual will be to try to evade tax. Models of this sort, although they are generally not based on any empirical evidence, do tend to suggest some factors which may influence the scale of tax evasion. On the one hand, tax evasion would tend to be encouraged by high rates of tax, because the financial savings from evasion would be correspondingly greater. On the other hand tax evasion would be discouraged the higher the risk of being caught, and the greater the punishment meted out to those who get caught. Similar considerations may also affect the level of benefit fraud.

Clearly though, a 'rational' calculation of this sort is likely to be only one of the elements which will enter into a decision by any particular individual to evade tax. The moral attitude of the individual towards tax evasion may also be important, as well as the moral attitudes of other family members, social pressures, the psychological ability to rationalise or 'excuse' personal acts of law-breaking and so on.

In addition the opportunities to evade tax will differ for different individuals. Some people may find that their work, or their social life, brings them into contact with opportunities for casual work which can be concealed from the tax authorities. Others, such as the self-employed, may find that their work gives them more control over their tax affairs than the majority of the working population, whose income tax is deducted at source by their employers. Particular skills and occupations may be in demand in the 'black economy', and particular parts of the country may have higher levels of demand for 'black economy' goods and services than others. Considerable variation would therefore be expected in the levels of tax evasion by different sections of the population, reflecting differences in the opportunities open to them.

In both Britain and Germany a sharp contrast can be drawn between those taxpayers who pay income tax through a withholding mechanism, and those who are, themselves, responsible for their own tax payments. In Britain the Pay-As-You-Earn (PAYE) system of income tax payment covers all employees (except for those with weekly earnings below a very low threshold, currently £38.50 per week), but not the self-employed. The latter group, who constitute about 10 per cent of income tax payers, are required to submit an income tax return to the authorities, and are then assessed and sent a bill for the tax due. Both because of the advantages of paying tax in arrears, and because of the greater scope for evasion that arises outside the PAYE system, it is necessary for the Inland Revenue to police the boundary between 'employee' and 'self-employed' status. In addition, certain arrangements have been introduced to tax some groups of self-employed workers (eg agency workers, and some sub-contractors in the building industry) through withholding arrangements similar to those for employees. Tax withholding arrangements are also applied to most investment incomes, including interest and dividends.

In Germany similar arrangements are in force. Withholding tax is levied at source for employee incomes, and the withholding tax also applies to certain kinds of domestic investment incomes. Self-employed taxpayers paying by self-assessment are required to make advance payments of tax every three months; the rest has to be paid (or the surplus repaid) after the declaration of income, which has to be made in the first half of the following year. About 15 per cent of income taxpayers pay through self-assessment in Germany.

Comparisons of the incentives for evasion provided by the structure of income and other taxes in Britain and Germany are made difficult by the complexity of the tax and social insurance systems in each country. The most direct incentive for evasion of income tax is likely to be the marginal rate of income tax, in other words, the additional tax that a taxpayer would have to pay out of an extra pound of earnings. In the UK this currently starts at 29 per cent ('the basic rate') for the vast majority of taxpayers; fewer than 4 per cent of taxpayers pay tax at higher rates, up to 60 per cent. The basic rate has been broadly stable for many years, but since the war there has been a considerable expansion in the number of people subject to income tax. This broadening of the coverage of income tax has been one factor in a steady rise in evasion incentives; a second has been the sharp rise in income-related National Insurance contributions. These were introduced in the 1960s; for most taxpayers they currently stand at 9 per cent of wages for employees, and a further 11.45 per cent paid by employers. (See Figure 2.2).

Figure 2.2   Marginal rates of income tax and compulsory social insurance contributions. Taxpayer at average manual earnings, Britain and Germany.

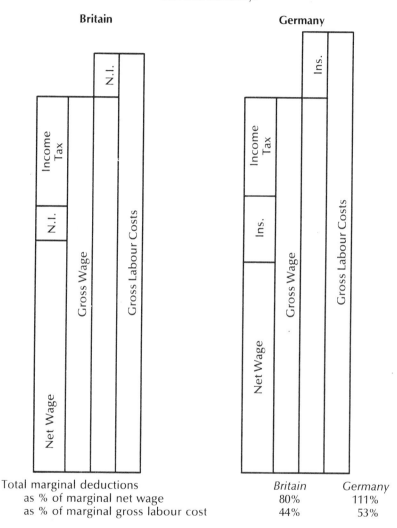

Total marginal deductions	*Britain*	*Germany*
as % of marginal net wage	80%	111%
as % of marginal gross labour cost	44%	53%

In Germany the marginal rate of income tax is 22 per cent over a range of annual incomes between DM4,537 and DM18,000 for a single person (for married single-earner couples the thresholds are double these levels), but the progressive element in income taxation affects the marginal rate at a much lower level of income in Germany than in Britain. Between annual incomes of DM18,000 and DM130,000 (for a single person) the marginal rate of income tax rises from 22 per cent to 56 per cent. At average manual earnings the marginal tax rate on an additional DM1,000 of earnings for a married man in Germany is about 26 per cent; compulsory social insurance contributions add further deductions of about 18 per cent of wages for the employee and the same for the employer. (Figure 2.2).

The marginal rates of taxation shown in Figure 2.2 measure the incentive to evade tax on casual earnings, or through employer/ employee collusion to evade the withholding tax (PAYE) arrangements. Different incentives apply to the combined evasion of income and Value Added Taxes through 'off-the-books' business. In such evasion a portion of the turnover of a business is concealed from the value added tax administration, and the corresponding labour costs and profits concealed from the income tax authorities. (In Britain VAT and income tax are administered by completely separate bodies, VAT by HM Customs and Excise and income tax by the Inland Revenue; in Germany merely by different tax offices.) Figure 2.3 shows a hypothetical illustration of the gains from tax evasion through 'off-the-books' business in Britain and Germany. Two types of business are compared. The first has a low ratio of materials purchased to turnover, and might be typified by a labour-intensive service provided to private households — painting and decorating perhaps. The second has a high level of material inputs to turnover — and might be taken to represent a retail business. Declaring the turnover of the business for VAT allows the VAT paid on inputs to be reclaimed; in the case of the retail business this sharply reduces the gains from evasion as a percentage of turnover. In both cases, if the proprietor of the business can appropriate all the gains from evasion, a substantial incentive to evasion through off-the-books business exists. However, if it is necessary to provide customers with a discount on the selling price in order to induce them to accept 'off-the-books' goods and services (eg to compensate them for the loss of legal redress or guarantees) the gains from off-the-books business in the second case will be much lower than in the first. For this reason it would be reasonable to expect that in both countries off-the-books business would be more common amongst businesses providing labour-intensive services than amongst retail businesses.

Figure 2.3   Evasion gains from "Off-the-books" transactions: two hypothetical businesses

BRITAIN	Business 1		Business 2	
	High value-added (eg painting & decorating)		Low value-added (eg retail sales)	
	cost structure	potential tax savings	cost structure	potential tax savings
Purchased inputs (excl. VAT)	20	–3.0	80	–12.0
Employee labour costs	40	17.6	10	4.4
Proprietor's income	40	13.8	10	3.45
VAT	15	15.0	15	15.0
Selling price	115	43.4	115	10.85
Total evasion gain				
as % net proprietor's income		166%		166%
as % of selling price		38%		9%

W. GERMANY	Business 1		Business 2	
	High value-added (eg painting & decorating)		Low value-added (eg retail sales)	
	cost structure	potential tax savings	cost structure	potential tax savings
Purchased inputs (excl. VAT)	20	–2.8	80	–11.2
Employee labour costs	40	21.2	10	5.3
Proprietor's income	40	14.8	10	3.7
VAT	14	14.0	14	14.0
Selling price	114	47.2	114	11.8
Total evasion gain				
as % net proprietor's income		187%		187%
as % of selling price		41%		10%

Note: Both comparisons show small unincorporated businesses not subject to corporation tax. "Tax" is, where appropriate, to be taken to include compulsory social insurance contributions. All figures relate to "marginal" incomes.

3 Measuring the Shadow Economy

The first step in measuring the size and economic importance of the shadow economy is to define clearly what is to be measured. As we have seen, there are a wide range of different activities included under the umbrella term 'shadow economy'. There are also a range of measurable aspects of these activities: the amounts of tax lost through evasion; the amount of value added in concealed activities; the amounts of income earned by tax-evaders; the amount of value added not reflected in the national accounts, etc. But, as Grass (1984) has observed, the authors who propose ways of measuring the shadow economy have up to now reached no clear consensus of what it is that they actually want to measure.

Rarely, of course, is there any confusion between measurement of the black economy, and measurement of the self-service economy, including household production, etc. The two phenomena are in many ways clearly distinct, and the measurement attempts have followed very different approaches. It is amongst the various estimates of the size of the black economy, in particular, that the greatest confusion has arisen.

Measurement of the black economy

Figure 3.1 shows the great range of measurement methods that have been applied to the black economy. Figure 3.2 summarises the

Figure 3.1   Measurement of the Black Economy

DIRECT METHODS	SURVEYS (Allensbach)	
	INFORMATION FROM TAX AUTHORITIES, ETC (IRS)	

INDIRECT METHODS	INDICATORS	DISCREPANCY BETWEEN TAX STATISTICS AND NATIONAL ACCOUNTS (Petersen)	National accounts methods
		INCOME: EXPENDITURE DISCREPANCIES MACRO (MacAfee) MICRO (Dilnot and Morris)	
		LABOUR MARKET (Contini, Langfeldt)	
		CASH CIRCULATION (Gutmann)	
		LARGE NOTES (Freud)	Monetary methods
		TRANSACTIONS METHOD (Feige)	
	CAUSAL MODELS	DEMAND FOR CASH (Tanzi)	
		DETERMINANTS/ INDICATORS (Frey)	

results of German studies; Figure 3.3 summarises studies for the UK.

A primary distinction might be drawn between direct and indirect measurement methods.

Direct Methods are based on direct observation of black economy activities either through surveys of participants, or from official sources, such as taxpayer audits. **Indirect Methods** proceed from the 'traces' that the black economy leaves elsewhere in the economy to infer the scale of black economy activities.

Many authors (including Frey and Pommerehne, 1982) pay little attention to the scope for direct measurement, believing that the need for secrecy by participants in the black economy makes direct measurement impossible, or at very least, highly unreliable. On the other hand, whilst indirect methods are less likely to be affected by the attempts of people evading tax to hide what they are doing, it is often difficult to assess whether the results from indirect methods

Figure 3.2   Estimates of the size of the black economy in Germany

Method	Year	Black economy as % of GDP	Reference	Coverage
Survey	1974	3.6	IfD Allens-bach (1975)	Paid work in spare time
National Accounts Discrepancies	1961 1968 1971 1974	16.0 12.6 6.5 4.8	Petersen (1982)	Incomes associated with tax evasion
	1968	8.9	Albers (1974)	
Labour market	1970 1976 1978 1980	(22) (39.5) (37.5) (35)	Langfeldt (1982)	Potential rise in labour supply in black economy
Transactions method	1965 1970 1976 1978 1980	3 16 17.5 24 27.5	Langfeldt (1982)	Cash and cheque transactions
Cash demand	1965 1970 1975 1980	4.3 3.1 6.0 10.3	Kirch-gässner (1982)	Cash transactions in black economy, due to increasing tax and social security burdens
	1976 1978 1980	12.1 11.8 12.6	Langfeldt (1982)	
Determinants/ Indicators	1978	8.3	Weck (1982)	?

Sources: Langfeldt (1983, p70), Langfeldt (1984, p187), Kirchgässner (1983, pp211, 213), Schrage (1984, p32). The final column represents our own assessment of the coverage.
nb. Figures in brackets are in no way comparable with the other figures.

Figure 3.3   Estimates of the size of the black economy in Britain

Method	Year	Black economy as % of GDP	Reference
National Accounts	1968	1½	MacAfee (1980)
Discrepancies	1973	2	
	1978	3½	
Cash demand	1973	2.9	Matthews
	1978	7.0	(1983)
	1983	15.9	
	1968	10.9	
	1973	13.3	Matthews and
	1978	14.1	Rastogi (1985)
	1983	14.5	
Transactions Method	1968	11	Feige (1981)
	1973	18	
	1978	14	
Household Income: Expenditure Discrepancies	1977	2.3-3.0	Dilnot and Morris (1981)

have anything to do with the black economy, or whether the 'traces' observed might not have other, perfectly innocuous, explanations.

Direct evidence of the black economy based on surveys of participants can seek information from either the seller, or from the buyer, of black economy goods and services. A major survey of possible sellers of black economy goods and services was conducted in Germany in 1974 by the *Institut für Demoskopie Allensbach* (1975). The aim of this survey was to assess the extent of paid free-time work in Germany. The survey was of all paid free-time work, and did not separately distinguish legitimate, taxed, second jobs from those which were not legitimate, and involved either illegal activities or tax evasion. As a result it will have included some part of the formal economy, as well as black economy second jobs. Survey evidence of second job-holding is also available from a number of sources in the UK, including the regular Family Expenditure Survey and the General Household survey. (See Alden, 1981, and Brown, Levin, Rosa and Ulph, 1984 for a discussion of these sources). Again, these surveys cover all second jobs, and do not separately distinguish those in the formal economy from those in the black economy.

One reason why these surveys have not probed further into the issue of tax evasion in second jobs is the likely sharp fall-off in response rates that would result. It is unlikely that someone with a casual job which was not declared for tax would be willing to admit their tax evasion to an official interviewer, and even academic researchers are likely to encounter some suspicion.

Whether a survey of customers in the black economy faces the same problems depends on the legal position of customers. In the UK, as in the USA, the black economy's customers are breaking no law themselves, and may well be quite co-operative with a survey of purchases in the black economy. Studies of informal service provision by Ferman and Berndt (1981) in Detroit, USA, and by Pahl (1984) in Sheppey, England, have been based on survey evidence from customers, and a small survey by Miller (1979) used the same approach. The problem is that customers may not always know that the person they are dealing with is evading tax; a request for cash payment, for example, is not a reliable touchstone of the black economy. At all events, this approach is of little use in Germany, where the laws to combat moonlighting make both the buyer and the seller guilty of an offence. In these circumstances, the buyer is just as likely as the seller to want to conceal the transaction.

The second kind of direct evidence of black economy earnings is that obtained from tax audits and other official investigations. A US study of this sort has been frequently cited (US Internal Revenue Service, 1979). This estimated the amount of unreported income in the USA, based on the Taxpayer Compliance Measurement Programme. The IRS uses information derived from detailed audits of selected taxpayers to analyse the characteristics of those who are likely to under-report income. The primary purpose is to facilitate computer selection of taxpayers for subsequent audit, but an incidental merit is the capacity to estimate the additional revenue which could be raised from all taxpayers if their affairs were subject to this degree of scrutiny. These calculations are supplemented by information derived from the Exact Match File, a compilation of several sources of government information on a group of 50,000 households, which allows estimates of income obtained by those who fail to make any return of incomes. The IRS conclusion is that between 91 and 94 per cent of income from legal sources is reported to it.

The under-recording of six to nine per cent found in this exercise is partly attributable to taxpayers claiming deductions which do not survive detailed scrutiny. (See Buttler, 1983, p27). About one third of the under-recorded income arises from this source — ie from erroneous calculation of net taxable income, rather than from understatement of gross income. This source of under-reporting does not have any direct relationship to the definition of the 'black economy' used by other studies. It also has no obvious counterpart in countries such as the UK and Germany where taxpayers are required to report gross income; and it is also likely to reflect the fact that a particularly wide range of deductions against tax are allowable in the US. No similar exercise has been conducted in either the UK or Germany; in the UK the exercise would be impossible because the Inland Revenue's powers do not permit random investigation of taxpayers, and in Germany too there is no legal basis for such an investigation.

Indirect estimates of the size of the black economy can be classified in a number of ways. The main classification used in Figure 3.1 distinguishes methods based on indicators from methods based on causal models. Another classification might be based on the kinds of 'traces' used as a guide to black economy activities. Some methods are based on the traces left in monetary statistics; others on traces left in expenditure data; others on the traces left in the labour market. (This classification is employed by Frey and Pommerehne, 1982).

Traces in **expenditure data** can be analysed both at the macro-economic and at the microeconomic level; in other words, using data for the economy as a whole, and using data for individual households. At the macroeconomic level, the estimates are based either on discrepancies within the national accounts (eg for the UK, MacAfee, 1980), or on discrepancies between the national accounts and other statistical sources (eg for Germany, Petersen, 1982). At the microeconomic level, the estimates are based on discrepancies between the reported incomes and expenditures of individual households (eg Dilnot and Morris, 1981, and Smith 1986). This method is not possible with the available German data.

MacAfee (1980) describes the way that the national accounts are calculated in the UK, and how this can give rise to discrepancies which might be due to the black economy. GDP is estimated from two largely independent data sources; an expenditure measure of GDP is estimated from survey data of expenditures, whilst an income measure of GDP is estimated from the amounts of income that taxpayers declare to the Inland Revenue. In theory, the two measures of GDP should be the same. Assuming that the expenditure figures are largely accurate, but that due to tax evasion the income figures understate the true level of income, the discrepancy between the two may be interpreted as the level of factor income in the black economy. In the UK this discrepancy, the 'initial residual difference' peaked at about 5 per cent in the mid-1970s, but has since fallen sharply, to the point where the income measure of GDP now exceeds the expenditure measure.

In Germany, a similar comparison is not possible, since the published statistics are adjusted in line with each other. Petersen (1982) has proposed an alternative method, based on a comparison of tax statistics with the German national accounts. The level of taxable income is adjusted to 'add back' deductions and allowances (although this is made difficult by the complexity and frequent changes of tax legislation), and then compared with the income measure of GDP. The results suggested that 16 per cent of income involved tax evasion in 1961, declining to 5 per cent in 1974. The main problem, of course, with both this method and MacAfee's estimates for the UK, is the impossibility of distinguishing discrepancies due to the black economy from discrepancies due to the inevitable statistical errors in the national accounts. As Hamer (1970) makes clear, there are plenty of ways in which the latter can arise.

The concept of black economy 'income' measured by the macro discrepancy approaches includes only concealed factor incomes (since it is factor incomes which are measured by the national accounts). Micro discrepancy measures, on the other hand, are directed at all forms of concealed household income, including concealed transfer payments. Dilnot and Morris (1981) compared the incomes and expenditures of the 7,000 households in the 1977 UK Family Expenditure Survey. This survey is a detailed expenditure survey, based on two-week diary records, with matching information on income and household circumstances. Dilnot and Morris found that some 10 or 15 per cent of households might have some form of concealed income, but that the total amount of hidden income was not large — equivalent to less than 3 per cent of GDP.

The obvious criticism of these estimates is that the survey is a voluntary survey, and that people with high levels of income in the black economy are unlikely to respond to the inquiry, for fear that their answers might somehow be communicated back to the tax authorities. This is not a trivial problem. Self-employed people are under-represented amongst respondents to the FES, and as Chapter 5 will show there are indications that they are particularly heavily involved in the black economy. Nevertheless, the response rate (about 70 per cent) to the FES is higher than for many other voluntary surveys, and Dilnot and Morris believe that although people engaged in large-scale tax fraud are unlikely to reply to the survey, many people with small-scale earnings in the black economy are likely to be included. Again, in Germany a similar approach is not applicable, for two reasons: the micro data from household surveys are not readily available, and the data are in any event partly adjusted to eliminate observed discrepancies between incomes and expenditures.

Traces left by the black economy in the **labour market** have been used to assess the scale of the black economy in Italy (eg by Contini, 1981). The 'participation rate' of the adult population in paid employment has varied considerably over the past few decades, both with the increasing participation of women in the labour force, and with growing unemployment. Some part of these changes in participation in final employment may have been due to changes in the level of black economy activity; what appears as a rise in unemployment might instead be a switch away from formal employment to employment in the black economy. Similarly, differences in participation rates between countries could be due to differences in the size of the black economy. Nevertheless, it is clear that there are many factors — including, in recent years, conjunctural factors — affecting participation rates, and to attribute changes in participation rates solely (or even partly) to the black economy has no justification. We concur strongly with Buttler's view that the use of participation rates to quantify the shadow economy is 'the most implausible' of all measurement methods. (Buttler, 1983).

Other candidates for this dubious accolade are to be found amongst the measurement methods based on 'traces' in **currency circulation**. A wide range of currency indicators have been suggested at various times. Most are based on the assumption that transactions in the black economy are made in cash, rather than by cheque, or by other means of payment which leave written evidence of the transaction. This assumption can, in itself, be questioned. In addition, the use of currency in the formal economy has undergone radical changes in the past two decades. Innovations such as credit cards, and the application of new technology (automatic bank tellers, etc) have revolutionised payments practices in many areas. It is hard to take seriously studies which try to interpret changes in currency circulation as evidence of changes in the black economy, without considering the major changes in payments practices that have an undoubtedly taken place.

Gutmann's (1977) estimates for the USA in his article 'The subterranean economy' attracted wide attention. These estimates were based on the relative rates of growth of currency in circulation and demand deposits since 1937-41 (which was chosen as the reference period). 'As black markets and tax avoidance mushroomed, currency shot up faster than demand deposits' (Gutmann 1977, p26), and by 1976 the black economy in the USA had reached at least 10 per cent of GDP. Criticism of these estimates has centred on the arbitrary choice of reference period (eg. Weck, 1982, p394) and also on the fact that changes in the ratio of cash to demand deposits actually appear to be due to changes in the use of demand deposits rather than in the use of cash (Tanzi, 1982). At all events, when applied to the UK and to Germany, Gutmann's method shows a rapid contraction of the black economy! (Smith, 1986, and Langfeldt, 1983).

Freud (1979) drew attention to the rapid rise in circulation of high-denomination notes in the UK over the period 1972-1978. These notes, he argued, were being used instead of cheques for large-scale black economy transactions. In Germany too the circulation of DM500 and DM1,000 notes has tripled between 1975 and 1981. However, O'Higgins (1980) and the Bank of England (1982) for the UK and Langfeldt (1983) for Germany point out that the increase in the number of high denomination notes in circulation can easily be accounted for by inflation.

Feige's estimates (1979 for the USA, 1981 for the UK) are based on a method which bears some resemblance to the currency methods, although they do not assume that black economy transactions are made exclusively in cash. Feige assumes that a stable relationship should exist between the volume of transactions and national income. On the basis of estimates of changes in the volume of transactions (based among other things on estimates of the velocity of circulation of currency, derived from scrapping rates and estimates of the physical durability of currency) Feige obtains independent estimates of the true level of national income, which in recent years appear to lie considerably above the level recorded in official statistics. Using Feige's method, Langfeldt (1983) obtained similar results for Germany, but he recorded strong reservations about the assumptions underlying the method.

The final currency method is one of the two 'causal' measurement approaches shown in Figure 3.1. Tanzi (1980) attempts a statistical explanation of the demand for money in terms of two groups of possible causal factors. The first group are the 'conventional' influences on the demand for money — the opportunity cost of holding currency, the levels of real income and prices, etc. The second group are factors such as tax rates, which may have affected the level of black economy activity, and hence, indirectly, the demand for money. By calculating what the demand for money would have been if these second factors have remained constant at a base-period level, Tanzi infers the growth in demand for money due to changes in the black economy since the base-period, and from this infers the growth in the level of black economy output since the base-period. Similar 'causal' estimates of the size of the black economy, based on the demand for currency, have been made for Germany by Kirchgässner (1982) and Langfeldt (1983), and for the UK by Matthews (1983) and Matthews and Rastogi (1985).

Overall, we must record our considerable scepticism about the value of estimates of the size of the black economy based on currency in circulation. As Tanzi (1982) has pointed out, selective use of monetary indicators can suggest a much higher level of black economy activity than is implied by any other measurement method. Dilnot and Morris (1981) observe that an equally selective choice of monetary indicators could show the black economy falling sharply in the UK, from 34% of GDP in 1952 to 7% in 1979. Kirchgässner's (1982 and 1983) estimates for Germany based on Tanzi's methodology show considerable sensitivity to the precise form of the equations and variables used. From those of his cash equations including a statistically significant co-efficient on the tax variable, twenty-six different estimates of the size of the black economy can be derived. The two 'best' equations show much the same figures, but around them there is a wide variation in the estimated size of the black economy:-

1960	between	0.1% and	2.5% of GDP
1965		2.2	4.4
1970		1.1	4.9
1975		1.9	8.6
1980		5.9	14.6

It is not always the same equation which yields the lowest and highest estimates. The estimates are, moreover, sensitive to the estimation period: those based on data for 1955-1980 tend to be higher than those based on the slightly longer period from 1952 to 1980.

The second 'causal' measurement approach has been developed by the research group of B.S. Frey (see, for example, Weck-Hannemann, 1984; Weck, Pommerehne and Frey, 1984; and Frey and Weck-Hannemann, 1984). The starting points for this approach are the 'causes' of the shadow economy, such as:-

- the tax burden
- decline in taxpaying morality
- the burden of government regulations
- disposable per capita income
- decline in the participation rate (of male workers)
- length of the working week
- perception of the tax burden
- unemployment rate.

Indicators for these various possible influences on the black economy are developed, but because there are no measures of the size of the black economy, their influence on the black economy cannot be tested, as would be done in conventional econometric research. Instead two methods are developed which are intended to show the (relative) size and evolution of the shadow economy. The first method rests on 'soft modelling', an approach which involves assigning 'plausible' weights to the possible influences on the shadow economy, and assessing the implications for the rate of growth of the shadow economy of these weights and of changes over time in the assumed determinants of the shadow economy. As Weck-Hannemann and Frey (1985, p97) acknowledge, the method 'rests on the assumption that the relevant causal variables have been correctly identified and that the weighting scheme used is reasonable ... the method only allows comparative statements ... but does not allow one to state what the size of the shadow economy is in percent of official GNP.'

The second method tries to relate some of the possible causes of the shadow economy to a number of variables which are believed to be indicators of its size. In Frey and Weck-Hannemann (1984) a comparison is made across 17 OECD countries, using indicators of 'official' GDP and labour market indicators (participation rates) to show the relative size of the shadow economy in each country, and four groups of possible determinants of the level of shadow economy activities. Causes and indicators are then statistically related using the LISREL procedure (Jöreskog and Van Thillo, 1973).

Both methods tread dangerously close to assuming what is to be measured, namely that rising tax rates, etc have led to a growth in the shadow economy in recent years. In addition, the second method appears to have only a tenuous relationship to the shadow economy; the supposed indicators of the shadow economy relate to the shadow economy only indirectly. The existence of a statistically significant relationship between causes and indicators could easily arise for reasons quite unconnected with the shadow economy.

Measurement of the self-service economy

The problems of measuring the black economy are largely the consequence of concealment. This is far less of a difficulty in measuring the self-service economy. On the other hand, a new and equally intractable problem arises — that of valuation.

The output of the household economy, and of voluntary organisations is generally not traded — and cannot, therefore, be valued by the prices at which it changes hands. A similar problem arises in valuing the output of many government services which are provided free of charge; in the national accounts such services are valued from the input side, by adding up the cost of the labour, materials, etc used in their production. This solution is not immediately available for the household economy, where one major input, the labour time of family members, is provided free.

Measurement approaches for the household economy's production focus on ways of attaching a value to the unpaid domestic labour input, so as to be able to value the output of household production by adding up the value of inputs used. Figure 3.4 shows that two broad approaches have been taken to valuation: the opportunity cost principle, and the market cost principle.

Figure 3.4   Measurement of the self-service economy

TIME BUDGET METHODS	OPPORTUNITY COST VALUATION OF LABOUR TIME (Nordhaus, Tobin)	
	MARKET COST VALUATION OF LABOUR TIME	SINGLE REPLACEMENT PERSON (eg domestic servant) (Eisner)
		WAGES FOR INDIVIDUAL ACTIVITIES (Hilzenbecher)
INSTITUTIONAL CARE COSTS (Clark)		

The opportunity cost approach sets the value of work done at home equal to the income the person could earn from alternatively spending the time working in the formal economy. It can be seen to derive from the model of time-allocation outlined by Becker (1965). This model leads to the conclusion that a rational individual will allocate the time available between household production, paid work in the formal economy, and leisure so that the marginal utility from time in each allocation is the same. The opportunity cost approach extends this result to the further conclusion that the value of the marginal hour's household production is equal to its oppor-tunity cost — in other words, equal to what could be earned from an hour's additional employment in the formal economy. This relationship, which is strictly only true at the margin, is then used to value all time spent on household production.

The market cost valuation principle uses the cost of employing someone else to do household work as a measure of the value of the goods and services produced. There are two variants of this approach: one calculates the cost of employing a single person (domestic servant) to replace the household members' own labour over the whole range of activities, the other calculates the cost of employing specialist labour to do each individual task (a cook to do the cooking, a handyman to do the DIY, etc). Both, in general, judge the scale of the task by the amount of labour time put in by the household members; in other words, it is assumed that household members are as productive as paid labour. In some areas of activity, such a DIY, this may be doubtful.

A more fundamental objection, raised by Hawrylyshyn (1977), to both valuation methods, is that at least some work in the household economy may be done for pleasure, as much as for the output that might result. In the case of the market cost approach this is a reason for assuming that the 'equal productivity' assumption is false. In the case of the opportunity cost approach the value of the own labour input is then no guide to the value of the output. (The more so because we are trying to measure the market value of specific goods and services in a way that is comparable with similar goods and services produced in the formal economy, rather than to measure utility or welfare.) At the very least, both valuation approaches need to be treated with caution.

Figure 3.5 summarises the results of the various attempts that have been made to measure the self-service economy in Germany. A rather different approach was taken in the one attempt that has been made to measure the value of household services in the UK. Clark (1958) based his estimates on statistics of the cost of upkeep for children and adults in institutional homes; he concluded that the aggregate value of household services in the UK in 1956 was equivalent to about one-third of measured UK gross national product.

Accuracy of the Estimates

A considerable margin of error surrounds all estimates of the scale of concealed transactions, and of the value of non-market production. As a result, both the estimates of the size of the shadow economy in Germany in the next chapter and the estimates of the scale of similar activities in Britain in the chapter following should be regarded merely as indications of orders of magnitude. We make no claims for any great precision in the estimates. Nonetheless, we believe that the estimates are a reasonable reflection of the relative sizes within each country of the shadow economy and the formal economy, and of the importance of different parts of the shadow economy.

Figure 3.5   Estimates of the size of the self-service economy in Germany

Method	Year	Size, as % GDP	Author	Coverage
Time budgets of private households, valued:				
with wage of home-help	1958	34 - 45 a)	Schmucker (1961)	housewives' work
with wage of single replacement person	1961	38	Adatia (1980)	total household production
	1971	38		
	1977	26 b)		
with opportunity cost (industrial worker)	1961	37.5	Langfeldt (1984; Daten = Adatia)	
	1971	44		
	1977	48.5		
with wage of single replacement person (female industrial worker)	1964	26.7-37.7		
	1970	24.9-37.8		
	1974	22.7-38.7		
	1980	21.9-41.4		
with opportunity cost (male industrial worker)	1964	37.1-52.5	Schettkat (1983)	housework/shopping
	1970	34.0-51.7		
	1974	30.0-51.3		
	1980	28.6-54.2		
with wages for individual activities	1982	52 - 68	Hilzenbecher (unpublished)	housework
Time budgets for honorary duties, valued at wage of industrial worker	1977	0.3-0.4	Langfeldt (1984)	only a small part of certain honorary duties in welfare organisations

a) as % of net domestic product at factor cost
b) as % of value added in all economic activities

Sources: See Figure 3.2

The Shadow Economy in Britain and Germany

However, the margin of uncertainty is sufficiently large to make it harder to draw firmly-based conclusions about the relative import- ance of the shadow economy in Britain and Germany. To take merely one example, the figures about the extent of second job- holding in the UK show a wide range, from 3 per cent in one survey to nearly 12 per cent in another. The differences between surveys can be interpreted in terms of differences in the precise question asked and differences in survey methodology; it is thought that some survey techniques were more likely to persuade people to reveal details of their second jobs than others. Nevertheless, whilst this interpretation can be put on the differences in the results from superficially similar UK surveys, it is evident that a substantial margin of uncertainty remains, even about something as apparently straightforward as the extent of second job holding in a single country. It is clear that the comparability of similar figures between Britain and Germany will be much harder to assess, and will, in general, be much more doubtful. Indeed, we do not believe that it is possible from the estimates we have made to say with any certainty whether the black economy or other aspects of the shadow economy in Britain are larger or smaller than in Germany.

Despite this rather pessimistic conclusion, we have nevertheless felt it worthwhile to organise the discussion of the shadow economy in Germany in the next chapter in such a way that it can be compared with the subsequent analysis for Britain. We believe that there are indeed insights to be gained from a comparison of the analyses of Britain and Germany. In the first place, there are interesting differences in research methodology, partly dictated by the information available in the two countries. Secondly, there are some marked differences in the perception of the shadow economy in the two countries, and in the legal and institutional framework, which are highlighted by our attempt to organise the research results for the two countries on a comparative basis. We believe that it is more likely to be in these respects, rather than in the size of the shadow economy, that the most important differences between the shadow economy in Britain and Germany are to be found.

4 The Shadow Economy in the Federal Republic of Germany

Petry and Wied-Nebbeling (1986) begin with some broad estimates of the possible scale of the shadow economy in Germany, based on the analysis of household 'time budgets'. These estimates are not intended to be precise measurements of the shadow economy, but instead indicate the broad orders of magnitude of shadow economy activities in relation to the formal economy and to other, non-productive, activities.

The output of the shadow economy is a function of the amount of labour time in the shadow economy, and of its productivity. Whilst time budget data provides a basis for assessing labour inputs to the shadow economy, it is hardly possible even to hazard a guess about the productivity of labour in the shadow economy. For this reason, the broad estimates of the size of the shadow economy made here are based on statistics of labour inputs only; no attempt is made to translate these into estimates of shadow economy value added.

'Time budget' data provides a broad indication of the amounts of time which the average German citizen devotes to various activities: to sleep, eating and other 'physical necessities'; to work in the formal economy; and to recreation. Figure 4.1 shows some rough estimates for 1981 of the use of time by German citizens over the age of 14. These estimates are based on a sample survey by the

The Shadow Economy in Britain and Germany

Figure 4.1   Average weekday time-use

German adult population

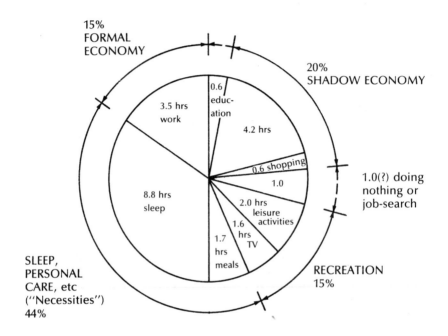

Source: Based on data in Petry and Wied-Nebbeling (1986), page 92

Allensbach Institute for IAW, reported in Keller (1984), and some estimates by Darkow (1982). On an average day the average German spent about 8.8 hours asleep, and a further 1.7 hours eating. Work in the formal economy accounted for about 3.5 hours, and education 0.6 hours. 3.6 hours were spent on recreational activities (including 1.6 hours watching television). Of the remaining 5.8 hours, 0.6 hours were spent shopping (which arguably falls midway between a recreational activity and a productive activity!), and unknown amounts of time were spent on job-search by the unemployed, and on aimless activity ('just doing nothing').

Supposing about an hour were devoted to these unquantified activities, this would leave around four hours a day which would include work in the shadow economy. This figure may seem on the high side, but it should be remembered that it contains the whole range of productive activities in the shadow economy, covering not merely 'moonlighting' in the black economy, but also legal productive activities in the household economy (cooking, cleaning, child-care, DIY, gardening etc) and in voluntary organisations. In the absence of detailed survey information about exactly how these four hours are spent, it is difficult to be definitive about the amount of labour devoted to the shadow economy. But from the Allensbach survey it is known that 2.3 hours are spent on housework and 0.6 hours on DIY (including repairs and sewing). There thus remain 1.3 hours for gardening, for activities in clubs and voluntary organisations, and for working in the black economy. In total, therefore, the estimate of about four hours devoted to the full range of shadow economy activities may not be too high.

The size of the black economy

The black economy contains a range of legal and illegal productive activities involving tax evasion and evasion of social insurance contributions. The greatest interest focuses on *Schwarzarbeit* ('black work'), against which specific legislation has been introduced in Germany. Other aspects of the black economy which are considered by Petry and Wied-Nebbeling (1986) are tax evasion on non-work incomes (rent, loans, etc), 'off-the-books' trading, the illegal loan of employees, and the illegal employment of foreign workers.

According to the German 'Law to combat *Schwarzarbeit*', three actions constitute offences against Paragraph 1:
- The concealment of productive activity by recipients of unemployment benefits
- The establishment of an unregistered business
- Carrying on a manual trade in a self-employed capacity without holding the appropriate qualifications

In addition, for an offence to have been committed, it is necessary for goods and services to have been produced, leading to significant economic gains.

The legislation thus encompasses hidden work by the unemployed, and hidden self-employment. It does not include concealed work by employees, including concealed second job holding by employees. Such evasion of taxes and social insurance contributions by employers and employees is frequently included in what is popularly meant by *Schwarzarbeit*, and will be considered here too under this heading.

Separate estimates are made of the possible extent of *Schwarzarbeit* in three areas: firms specialising in *Schwarzarbeit*, concealed second job holding by employees, and hidden work by the unemployed. The estimates were made for 1983 wherever possible.

Firms specialising in *Schwarzarbeit*

Official bodies responsible for detecting *Schwarzarbeit* report that professional *Schwarzarbeiter* in manual trade occupations operate in the following ways: either the firm is not registered at all, or a firm is registered, but does a certain amount of its work 'off-the-books', without billing. Often, too, an otherwise 'clean' company may engage as a sub-contractor an unregistered tradesman, whose employees are not registered with either the taxation or social insurance authorities.

Two ways might be pursued of attempting to quantify the economic importance of businesses specialising in *Schwarzarbeit* in manual trade occupations. The first proceeds from the evidence available about prosecutions for this form of *Schwarzarbeit*, and, making assumptions about the percentage of companies which are detected, estimates the extent of detected and undetected company *Schwarzarbeit*. The second method is based on assessments by the public officials responsible for business registration of the number of unregistered businesses, and of their characteristics.

Offences against the law to combat *Schwarzarbeit* can lead to a fine of up to DM50,000; both the supplier and the customer are liable to prosecution. The fines aim to counter the economic gains from *Schwarzarbeit*, including both the wages of the *Schwarzarbeiter* and the savings made by the customer. Table 4.1 shows the total fines raised from convictions for *Schwarzarbeit* in various manual trade occupations in 1980 and 1983; the aggregate amounts raised were about DM6.5 million in 1983.

There is some evidence of a rising trend, both in money terms (a near-doubling between 1980 and 1983) and in relation to total declared turnover in the listed trades. How far this reflects a growing level of *Schwarzarbeit* is difficult to assess, since it could equally well

The Shadow Economy in the Federal Republic of Germany

Table 4.1   Fines for *Schwarzarbeit* in manual trades

	1980 DM 1000s	1980 % of turnover	1983 DM 1000s	1983 % of turnover
Bricklayers, concrete and reinforced concrete engineers, road builders	1,195	0.02	1,568	0.03
Painters and varnishers	487	0.05	715	0.07
Roofers	482	0.08	1,131	0.20
Motor mechanics	193	0.00	353	0.01
Central heating and ventilating engineers	137	0.01	175	0.02
Tiling, paving, mosaic layers	170	0.04	254	0.07
Plasterers	103	0.03	188	0.06
Gas and water installation, plumbers	176	0.02	228	0.02
Joiners	191	0.01	303	0.02
Structural cleaners	72	0.02	143	0.04
Locksmiths	68	0.01	165	0.01
Floor layers	62	0.05	71	0.06
Electricians	40	0.00	72	0.01
Other branches	516	0.00	1,118	0.01
Total, manual trades	3,890	0.01%	6,456	0.02%

Source: Petry and Wied–Nebbeling (1986), Tables 4 and 5

reflect the increased resources devoted to enforcement in recent years.

What might these figures suggest about the importance of *Schwarzarbeit* in these trades? A starting point might be the estimates made by a number of chambers of trade that about 10 per cent of cases of *Schwarzarbeit* are discovered. This is a broad assessment, which cannot necessarily be applied to individual trades. It is, moreover, difficult to assess how plausible a 10 per cent detection rate might be; the chambers of trade agree that most cases of *Schwarzarbeit* are discovered by accident, often as a result of complaints by dissatisfied customers, although some field investigation officers are employed.

Assuming that 10 per cent of cases are detected, and that the penalties levied in these cases exhaust the profits made from *Schwarzarbeit*, total profits by firms specialising in *Schwarzarbeit* would have been around DM65 millions in 1983. Assuming, further, that the average profits: gross value added ratio for small businesses employing two or three employees applies to firms specialising in *Schwarzarbeit*, each unit of profits corresponds to some 2.25 units of gross value added. In total, therefore, the value added by firms specialising in *Schwarzarbeit* could be around DM145 millions, equivalent to only about 0.1 per cent of the total gross value added in these trades. Even if the detection rate was only a tenth of that assumed, so that only one 'black' firm in a hundred was caught and prosecuted, value added by such firms would still amount to only one per cent of total value added in manual trades.

Similar, though slightly higher figures result from the second estimation method. According to an estimate by an informed official of the office responsible for business registration in Stuttgart, there were in addition to the 42,000 registered business enterprises in Stuttgart a further 10 per cent of unregistered businesses, operating in the black economy, with, in the main, only one or two employees. This estimate seems, if anything, rather high, since the business enterprises covered include many industrial, export, credit and insurance companies, and in these areas the black economy is likely to be rather small. Most black economy businesses would seem likely to be the building trades, cleaning and renovation, and some other manual trades.

In total, throughout the Federal Republic, there are some 320,000 registered businesses in these categories. If, in addition, there are a further 32,000 unregistered businesses, each employing on average two people, the black economy in this area could have an annual value added of some DM2,500 millions, or about 1.7 per cent of the reported turnover of all manual trades. This seems likely to be towards the top end of the possible range for production by companies specialising in *Schwarzarbeit* in trade occupations.

Concealed second job-holding

Second jobs may sometimes provide scope for concealment of earnings, particularly in relatively small-scale informal businesses, and amongst workers who have skills which are in demand from friends and neighbours (eg hairdressers, plasterers, etc). Consideration of the extent and pattern of second job holding may provide some indication of the amounts of income that could be concealed by second job holders. Such estimates are, inevitably, somewhat tentative; some second job holders, at least, will declare their secondary earnings for tax, and will make the appropriate social insurance contributions. Again, two methods are employed. The first is based on time-budget information about the amount of time spent working on second jobs, and the second makes some broad estimates of plausible orders of magnitude in occupations where concealed second job holding is likely to be prevalent.

The most recent survey containing information about the amount of time devoted to second jobs in Germany was conducted in November and December 1974 (*Institut für Demoskopie Allensbach*, 1975). A sample of around 4,000 adults, including people in employment, housewives, students and pensioners was asked whether they undertook paid work in their free time. 31% of respondents said that they frequently or regularly did such work. On an average day 7.5 per cent had done paid work in their free time, and on these occasions the average amount worked was about three hours. These figures would imply that across the population as a whole an average 80 hours of paid work was done per year in free-time occupations. Assuming average gross hourly earnings in second jobs of DM9, the 43.7 million Germans over the age of 15 might have produced DM31.5 billions-worth of value added in second jobs in 1974. Scaled up to 1983 prices and population figures this would be about DM55.4 billion, equivalent to some 3.6 per cent of GDP.

Naturally, these estimates are only approximate, and there is perhaps little point in attempting further refinements (such as, for example, adjusting the population totals to exclude the very old, and to bring in the possible output from second jobs held by foreigners resident in Germany). Owing to the time of year when the survey was undertaken the figures for second job holding may well be somewhat understated; there may be considerably more opportunities during spring and summer both in the tourist trade, and in 'outdoor' occupations such as construction and agriculture.

On the other hand, the figures are likely to overstate considerably the extent of *Schwarzarbeit* in second jobs. Skilled manual trades are often believed to be the area where the black economy is greatest. Yet only some 30 per cent of the men with second jobs in the Allensbach survey (and only 2 per cent of the women) had their second jobs in those areas. More significantly, the survey was not explicitly directed at the issue of concealed work, and did not ask the questions necessary to distinguish legitimate, taxed, second jobs, and free-time jobs not liable to tax, from *Schwarzarbeit* in second jobs. Quite a number of the jobs identified may well involve no liability to tax. For example, the survey included a range of people (pensioners, housewives, students) who may not have a regular job. For those people, tax liability on their free-time work begins only when their income exceeds a certain threshold. For Class I and Class IV tax payers (single people, and two-earner married couples) the liability to tax begins only when daily earnings exceed DM18.79, whilst liability to tax on secondary earnings for people holding two jobs (Class VI) begins at only DM0.19 daily. Similarly, the obligation to pay social insurance contributions only begins once earnings exceed a given threshold (DM390 per month in 1983, DM410 per month in 1986), or when more than 15 hours are worked per week. (See Marschall 1983, pp83,106ff). As a result, whilst most second jobs involve liability to tax, the small jobs held by housewives, pensioners and students may often not involve any tax or social insurance liability, and should thus not be counted as part of the black economy.

The second approach to estimating the scale of the black economy amongst second job holders is based on an assessment of the occupations most likely to be involved, and the hours that might be worked in second jobs. The aim is to delineate plausible orders of magnitude, rather than to make exact estimates.

The Allensbach survey mentioned above found that every second employee in the building industry was an intensive free-time worker, two-thirds of the free-time jobs being in trade occupations. As an upper limit to the amount of *Schwarzarbeit* done by building workers, we might assume that half the 413,000 workers in the main building trades are actively involved in the black economy, working on average an extra 20 hours a week (2 on weekdays, 10 on Saturdays) for eight months of the year. If we assume, further, that their average hourly earnings for this *Schwarzarbeit* are DM20, this would imply a total concealed value added of some DM2.6 billion, equivalent in 1983 to about 10 per cent of gross value added in the building industry as a whole. Similar assumptions for 'finishing' trades in the building industry would imply concealed value added of DM1.6 billion, nearly 15 per cent of declared value added in these trades. These are almost certainly maximum estimates, and may well be excessive. They would imply that one in every ten houses was built in the black economy by second job holders, quite apart from the further work done by firms specialising in the black economy, by unemployed building workers, by otherwise legitimate firms trading 'off the books', and through own-labour and the assistance of neighbours, besides the work done by legal construction firms.

Two other trades which are often mentioned in the context of the black economy are vehicle mechanics and hairdressers. In both occupations, however, the scope for second-job *Schwarzarbeit* is somewhat less than in the building industry. Vehicle repairs in the black economy may be limited by the need for work premises and tools; whilst small repairs, engine tuning and so on are likely to be feasible spare-time occupations, major repairs are less easily carried out on an informal basis. Assuming half the vehicle mechanics in Germany work four hours per week in 'black' second jobs, at an hourly rate of DM25, concealed value added might be DM570 millions, 1.3 per cent of declared turnover.

The limitation on second job holding in hairdressing arises from the high percentage of women in the trade. Owing to the double burden of job and household, women are likely to have less time to work in second jobs (except if their main job is part-time which is rare in hairdressing). If a quarter of hairdressing employees have second jobs for an average of four hours a week, at DM20 per hour, some DM190 million of value added would be involved, equivalent to some 3 per cent of industry turnover.

Cleaning is likely to offer considerable scope for concealed secondary employment, partly because of the lack of any need for training, and because much cleaning is done for private households 'cash-in-hand'. On the basis of the Allensbach survey, some 2.5 per cent of the female population have casual cleaning jobs. Assuming 3 hours per weekday, paid at DM10 per hour, would indicate upwards of DM2 billion concealed income in cleaning, quite apart from the illegal employment of foreigners in cleaning occupations (say a further DM0.3 billion), and off-the-books turnover of cleaning firms. Perhaps as much as 60 per cent of cleaning business could be in the black economy.

For other manual occupations the amounts earned in concealed second jobs may be lower — say, one in ten working four hours a week, at DM20 per hour implies a further DM6 billion of concealed value added. Taking all the manual occupations together, a total of DM13.3 billions (or 4 per cent of value added in manual trades) could be concealed in second jobs in manual trades.

Second jobs also exist outside manual occupations. Estimates suggest that some 5 to 10 million hours are lost each year through public officials working on their own account during paid time (Aberle and Eggenberger, 1979, pp199ff), although the incomes they earn from this work may not necessarily be concealed from the tax authorities. Teachers have many opportunities to provide extra coaching for cash-in-hand payment (an hour a week per teacher would yield some DM350 million additional income). Part time insurance salesmen too may be able to work 'cash-in-hand' (concealed income of perhaps DM50 millions).

In a wide range of other occupations there may be some occasional scope for supplementing regular earnings. Nevertheless, there is a considerable gap between the rough guesses made above, which total only about DM13.7 billion of concealed value added, and the corresponding estimate from the Allensbach survey of about DM55 billion. It does not seem plausible that outside the areas most frequently cited as prone to *Schwarzarbeit* something around three times as much concealed income could be earned as in the areas where the problem is believed to be greatest. For this reason the Allensbach estimate is likely to be an upper limit. One thing, however, is clear: despite all the uncertainties about estimation, *Schwarzarbeit* in second jobs appears to be far more significant in total than the activities of firms specialising in *Schwarzarbeit*.

It is to be noted that a part of the second job incomes concealed in order to evade tax may nonetheless be reflected in the national accounts statistics; for example, 'black' work done in legitimate firms and the illegal work done in the building industry will both be included, because of the way the statistics are compiled.

Hidden work by the unemployed

By law, people receiving unemployment benefit or assistance may earn up to DM15 per week without their benefit entitlement being affected. Earnings beyond this level result in a direct reduction in benefit payments (Marschall, 1983, pp133*ff*). Practically all the undeclared casual jobs of benefit recipients would thus form part of the black economy.

There is little information to go on about the extent of such jobs. There is merely a certain amount of information about detected areas of benefit abuse. Part of this derives from intensive investigations under Article 132 of the *Arbeitsförderungsgesetz* (Law to Encourage Work) of suspect business in various categories, including seasonal trades, businesses where wages are paid gross of income tax, etc. In the eighteen months between January 1984 and June 1985 13,182 companies with a total of 178,800 employees were investigated in the Federal Republic, and some 11,410 more or less serious cases of benefit abuse were discovered. On average the benefit overpayment was DM671 per individual, but there was considerable variation. A second method of detecting 'working and claiming' has been recently made possible by the introduction of a computer comparison between social insurance contribution records, and records of benefit payments. By this route some 71,150 cases of benefit abuse, involving average benefit losses of DM341 per case were discovered between January 1984 and March 1985. Nevertheless, whilst these figures demonstrate that a problem of benefit abuse exists, it is difficult to draw any inferences about the total scale of detected and undetected abuse from figures relating only to the amount of abuse detected.

There are, however, good reasons for believing that the scope for *Schwarzarbeit* by the unemployed is no greater than for people in employment. Whilst the unemployed may have considerable free time for casual work, they are likely to have more limited access to both the tools and the social contacts needed for work in the black economy. In addition, they are likely to encounter a certain amount of customer suspicion; customers may feel that a tradesman who has been able to find employment is more likely to be good at his (second) job than one who has not.

Some of the unemployed with trade qualifications may find black economy employment easier to come by. The 107,000 unemployed workers in the building trades (1983) may be able to find work more easily than unemployed people without qualifications. Supposing, for example, half of the 'unemployed' building workers were in fact, working for 20 hours a week, for eight months of the year, at an hourly wage rate of DM20, some DM680 million of concealed value added would be involved. Over all unemployed occupations the figures for average free-time work from the Allensbach survey might be used to suggest an upper limit: some 80 hours paid work annually by each of the 2.25 million unemployed in Germany in 1983, paid at DM15.40 per hour, would imply a total concealed income of DM2.8 billion, equivalent to 0.2 per cent of official GDP. (Some of these concealed incomes of the unemployed are already likely to be included in the GDP statistics.)

Other concealed incomes and illegal employment
There are a number of other possible sources of 'black' income for private households and individuals — eg:-
- rental incomes, income from loans, etc.
- tips
- barter
- untaxed criminal incomes
- prostitution.

Unfortunately, little information exists about the extent of concealed income in these categories — although plausible figures for tips in occupations such as hairdressing, the catering trade and taxi-driving suggest that the total amounts involved might be considerable (DM200 per month per person in these trades would total about DM1.5 billion per annum). In the case of criminal incomes information is, understandably, almost non-existent; in any event, there is a certain amount of doubt about whether criminal activities should be regarded as yielding 'value' added.

Further sources of concealed business income (and associated concealed employment) which may be significant include:-
- off-the-books trading
- illegal loan of employees
- illegal employment of foreigners.

Off-the-books trading (sales that are not billed, and that do not appear in the company accounts) are likely to occur to some extent in all lines of business. But there are two areas where off-the-books trading may be particularly important: in retail sales, and in manual trades. Both areas are characterised by a strong pressure of competition (in manual trades not least due to competition from moonlighters and DIY), and both involve a high percentage of sales to private households and individuals (who, unlike business customers, have in most cases no need for documentary evidence of purchases).

On the other hand, there are a number of factors which may tend to constrain the level of 'off-the-books' business. In the retail trade it is necessary to maintain a plausible level of sales in relation to purchases; only a certain percentage of the stock bought in can be written off as breakages or theft before the suspicion of the tax authorities is aroused. Similar factors will partially constrain the level of off-the-books business even in areas such as painting and decorating businesses.

From the customer's point of view, too, there may be disadvantages to 'off-the-books' goods and services. For example, the Guarantee on retail purchases is likely to be ineffective if no proof of purchase exists. In the case of building work, moreover, the scope for tax deductibility of costs up to DM200,000 - DM250,000 per new one- and two-family house, means that customers have no incentive to purchase 'off-the-books' work until those limits are exceeded.

There is only limited information about the extent of 'off-the-books' trading in Germany. Petry and Wied-Nebbeling (1986) present some evidence of different rates of turnover growth in different sections of the building industry and retail trade which might, amongst other factors, reflect growing off-the-books trading in certain areas. The overall value of such trade is unknown but could run into tens of billions of Deutsch Marks.

The problem of illegal lending of employees is concentrated in the building and the metal industries. Much of the illegal lending is of non-German employees. In the building industry, besides Yugoslav and Turkish workers (who are poorly paid), groups of Dutch and British workers (sometimes registered as unemployed at home) have been the subject of illegal lending arrangements. Much illegal lending of employees will be associated with evasion of tax and social insurance contributions, but any lending of employees without the permission of the *Bundesanstalt für Arbeit* is an offence. It is believed that as many as 100,000 employees (around 0.5 per cent of the total insured workforce) may be illegally lent from one employer to another.

Not all of the value added by such employees will necessarily be omitted from the national accounts. In the building industry the use of output indicators to measure production means that the work done by illegally-lent employees (along with the work done by *Schwarzarbeiter*) will be included, regardless of what employment is concealed by the businesses involved. In other industries, the work done by loaned employees may be included in the output of the lending firms (and thus may be measured by official statistics).

The illegal employment of foreigners is believed to be a much greater problem in terms of the numbers involved than is the problem of illegal employee lending. In 1980 the *Bundesanstalt für Arbeit* detected some 70,000 cases, and in 1983 more than 30,000. Many of these involved merely formal work permit infringements; in 1983 prosecution followed in only one-sixth of the detected cases.

The number of illegally employed foreigners is declining, partly as a result of the poor labour market situation, but also because over time more than 80 per cent of the foreign workers in the Federal Republic have, by virtue of the amount of time they have been working in Germany, established a legal claim to the necessary work permits. Nevertheless, there may still be some 200,000 to 300,000 foreigners seeking work illegally in Germany (*Deutscher Bundestag*, 1984, p34), generally at low wages, in small and medium-sized enterprises. Because of the way the statistics are calculated, however, most of the work done by illegally employed foreigners will be reflected in the national accounts; only if the business is unregistered will it be omitted (and it will then be a part of the figures discussed above, for the business of firms specialising in *Schwarzarbeit*).

The size of the self-service economy

The self-service economy comprises a wide range of productive activities, — including housework, DIY, activities in clubs and voluntary organisations, etc. These are considered separately under the following headings.

Housework

There have been a number of investigations into the amount of time devoted to housework in Germany (see Krautwald, 1982, and Dornach, 1982, for surveys of the evidence). The definition of housework is by no means clear, which makes it difficult to compare the existing studies. Table 4.2 summarises a number of time budget estimates for housework, which use similar definitions, but which were made at various times using different methods of investigation. There is a general tendency for the estimates based on diary records to be higher than those based on questionnaire surveys; but there is also a clear indication that over a number of years the amount of time spent on housework has declined.

Only the study by Hilzenbecher (1984), which reports a survey by the *Institut für Sozial- und Familienpolitik* at the University of Marburg, records a rise in housework compared to earlier studies employing the same method. Part of this can be explained by the inclusion in the survey of a very wide range of activities, some of which arguably might not be counted as part of housework. Taking these questionable categories out reduces the total from 58 hours per week to 53.7 hours per week per household, which is still a little above the level recorded in 1977.

Overall the figures in Table 4.2 suggest that somewhere between 42.2 billion hours (1980) and 67.9 billion hours of housework (1982) is done annually in the Federal Republic. The lower estimate receives some independent confirmation from time-and-motion studies of the time needed for housework, which suggest a daily requirement of 1.5 to 2 hours per person (see Dornach, 1982, p152, and Krautwald, 1982, p53), which grosses up to an annual requirement of up to 43 billion hours.

Some two-thirds of all household work is done by women. There is a considerable difference, however, between the amounts of time spent on household work by full-time housewives and working wives. Part of the difference may reflect the fact that when both partners work some household jobs (eg cooking midday meals) do not need to be done; but another factor may be a greater use of convenience foods and other labour-saving techniques by working women.

This process of substitution (substitution of formal economy convenience foods for home cooking, etc) may have implications not merely for the amount of household labour time, but also for the quality of output. There is no presumption that household production or formal economy alternatives are generally superior or inferior in quality. In some cases, the higher incomes of working wives may allow the purchase of higher quality goods and services.

Table 4.2   Time spent on housework

hours per week per household

Method	Source	Year	Housework times (including shopping and child-care)	
			Women only	all family members
Diary records	Krautwald[1]	1968/69	—	61.6
	Wild/Zander[2]	1972	—	58.0
	Krautwald[3]	1977	—	52.5
	Hilzenbecher[4]	1982	39.1	58.0
Questionnaire	Krautwald[5]	1972/74	60.0	—
	Darkow[6]	1980	—	34.0

Notes:

1. Diary records by 132 urban households (Krautwald, 1982)

2. Diary records by 10 farm households and 67 urban 4-person households in Baden-Württemberg (Wild and Zander, 1975)

3. Diary records of 134 participants at further education courses (Krautwald, 1982)

4. 1106 families in Baden-Württemberg: Institut für Sozial-und Familienpolitik, Marburg University (Hilzenbecher, 1984)

5. Three surveys in 1972-1974 by H. Pross (Krautwald, 1982)

6. Representative sample, population over 14 (Darkow, 1982)

The Shadow Economy in the Federal Republic of Germany

On the other hand, it may often be that people doing their own housework are more motivated to do it well.

It is thus extremely difficult to draw inferences about the value of household output from information about the amount of time spent on housework; quite apart from the time valuation problems noted in the previous chapter. Nevertheless, to illustrate the approximate scale of housework in relation to GDP, the hourly gross labour costs for household servants (DM13.30) might be applied to the estimated maximum and minimum household work totals, to yield total output values in 1983 of DM903 billion to DM572 billion, equivalent to between 59 per cent and 37 per cent of formal economy GDP respectively.

Do-it-yourself (DIY) work

The study by Ollmann, Niessen and Ehling (1985) found that DIY work was concentrated mainly in three areas:-
- home decoration/renovation
- building alterations and extensions
- servicing and repair of motor vehicles.

As Table 4.3 shows, wallpapering and painting are the most popular DIY tasks, but a considerable percentage of the population also undertake a wide range of other tasks. DIY is more common

Table 4.3   Percentage of population doing DIY tasks

Percentage of German population over 14, 1982

Activity	All	Men	Women
Wallpapering	55	68	44
Painting	54	68	43
Joinery, woodwork	20	33	9
Electrical installation	18	29	8
Other DIY tasks	25	32	18

Source: Media-Analyse 1981/82: taken from Gruner und Jahr AG & Co, editors, 1983, p8

amongst adults in their thirties and forties than amongst older and younger age groups. It is not restricted to any particular social class: one study (*Arbeitsgemeinschaft Rundfunkwerbung*, 1983) found that it was least common amongst senior managers, and most common amongst middle managers and officials. Another study (*Institut für Demoskopie Allensbach*, reported in Keller, 1984) found a somewhat different pattern of participation, with DIY most common amongst skilled manual workers (Table 4.4). The differences can most probably be attributed to differences in the employment classification and in the definition of DIY.

Table 4.4

DIY (incl. repair in house or flat, car maintenance, and sewing); Characteristics of participants

	FRG aged 14 and over percentage participation
men	81
women	71
all	76
age 14-19	56
age 20-29	78
age 30-39	82
age 40-49	84
age 50-59	81
age 60-69	77
age 70 and over	66
by socio-economic group	
self-employed	69
executives/senior public officials	78
other employees/public officials	75
skilled manual workers	81
other workers	71
farmers	76

Source: Keller (1984, p 172); own calculations

Table 4.5 summarises the results of a number of surveys of the amount of time spent on DIY work. The figures for 1969 and 1974 are not directly comparable, partly because in 1974 a greater range of activities was covered, and women were included in the survey. Comparing the figures for men aged between 16 and 69 only, there was a significant rise in the time spent on DIY, from about 70 hours in 1969 to 100 hours in 1974 (see Dornach, 1982, p165*ff*). Part of this at least may have reflected genuine growth in the time spent on DIY. The estimates for 1984 are broadly comparable with those for 1969 and 1974 in their coverage of DIY activities by men. They suggest a levelling-off in the rate of growth of DIY time since 1974. In 1969 a total of some 1.4 billion hours of DIY work was done by the German male population, in 1974 1.8 billion hours, and in 1984 1.9 billion hours.

Table 4.5   Time spent on DIY

hours per year

Survey date	Note	by active DIY workers	by survey respondents	by total population (estimate)
1969	(1)	—	70	1,370 m
1974	(2)	—	58	2,200 m
1978	(3)	100	—	—
1981	(4)	—	225	11,400 m
1981/82	(5)	—	150	7,600 m
1983	(3)	92	56	1,320 m
1984	(6)	—	110	1,870 m

Notes:

(1)   Men aged 16-69, survey by *GFK Nürnberg* (Dornach, 1982)

(2)   German population 16-69, survey by *GFK Nürnberg* (Dornach, 1982)

(3)   Surveys by *Institut für Freizeitwirtschaft, München*

(4)   Population over 14, wide DIY definition. Allensbach survey (Keller, 1984)

(5)   Population over 14, wide DIY definition. *Arbeitsgemeinschaft Rundfunkwerbung* (1983)

(6)   Head of household between 22 and 64 – building and renovation work only. (Ollmann, Niessen and Ehling, 1985)

The lack of any substantial growth in DIY labour in the late 1970s/early 1980s is confirmed by the two surveys by the *Institut für Freizeitwirtschaft*, for 1978 and 1983. Between 1978 and 1983 the number of people doing DIY (only so-called 'active' home-workers, ie people frequently engaged in DIY) rose from 10.8 million to 12.7 million, but the average amount of time worked by each person fell.

The foregoing surveys have largely been confined to home decoration and repair activities. A broader definition, including vehicle maintenance, sewing and some other activities was employed by the 1981 survey by the *Institut für Demoskopie Allensbach*. This found that the average German adult spent four and a half hours a week on DIY activities. Over a year this would imply a total DIY labour input of some 11.4 billion hours, well above the levels in the other studies.

A clear picture of the amount of time devoted to DIY is thus difficult to obtain; different surveys using somewhat different definitions yield markedly different results. These problems are further compounded by valuation difficulties. The time input to DIY may be little guide to the value of the output. Some DIY workers may, through inexperience, work much more slowly than professional painters, decorators and vehicle mechanics; others may work more carefully, and produce higher-quality output than professional workers. (See Dornach, 1982, p173). Petry and Wied-Nebbeling (1986) base their estimates of the value of DIY output on an opportunity cost valuation of the labour input (which avoids some of these productivity problems), and estimate that the total annual value of DIY output in Germany could be between DM100 and 150 billion, equivalent to between 6.4 and 9.6 per cent of GDP.

Other activities in the self-service economy

Amongst the many other activities where there may be substitution between the formal economy and the shadow economy, two are of importance: transport, and activities in clubs and voluntary organisations.

Each German over the age of 14 spends about half an hour a day in a private car, mainly in travel to work or going shopping. Not all of this private travel necessarily involves the creation of value added. Nevertheless, if all the private travel were to take place on public transport instead, it is clear that there would be a substantially higher level of net output in public transport industries. On the basis of the distance travelled in private cars, and the price per kilometer for public transport, the additional net output would be of the order of DM45 billions.

In the Federal Republic of Germany there is a long tradition of clubs and societies. Around 30 per cent of the population (19 million people or so) are organised into more than 70,000 clubs, including 58,000 sports clubs, and about 15,000 choral societies. (Gmelin, 1984, p216 and *Statistisches Jahrbuch*, 1984, pp388-9). According to Gmelin (1984) more than 1.5 million people hold some form of office in sports clubs, working perhaps on average about 4 hours per week on club business. (Gmelin notes that this time has been declining over a number of years). If this time were valued at the average net hourly wage, it would total perhaps DM3.9 billion per year.

In addition to club activities there are also the activities of self-help organisations. A study by the *Institut für Demoskopie Allensbach* estimated that in 1977 about 5 per cent of adult German citizens were active in voluntary organisations, working on average between 12 and 18 hours per month. Over a full year this would be some 288 - 432 million hours, which, if valued at DM13 per hour would imply a total value of between DM3.7 and DM5.6 billion.

Summary: The shadow economy in Germany

It should again be stressed that considerable uncertainty attaches to all our estimates of the scale of shadow economy activities; a number of them are little more than guesses about plausible orders of magnitude. Nevertheless, despite the uncertainties, a number of points emerge clearly.

In particular, our estimates show the overwhelming importance of the self-service economy in the total of shadow economy activities. The black economy may well produce less than 5 per cent of the output of the formal economy. Labour inputs to the self-service economy, on the other hand, probably exceed labour inputs to the formal economy (see Figure 4.1), and, whilst there are intractable valuation problems, the value of output from the self-service economy is evidently large in relation to formal economy GDP.

Whether the shadow economy in Germany is growing is harder to assess. Housework times have been declining over a number of years, partly because of the growing participation of women in the formal economy workforce. However, at the same time housework productivity has risen, reflecting the growing use of labour saving devices. The overall effect of these two trends on the output of the household economy is unclear.

DIY work may have increased in importance during the late 1960s and the 1970s but the subsequent growth has been less rapid. Nevertheless, further growth is to be expected. Industry commentators (eg. Gruner und Jahr AG & Co, eds, 1983) believe that growing unemployment may have boosted the amount of DIY work, and new tools and materials which make DIY easier are continually being developed. (This process implies that a growing DIY sector will also require some growth in industries in the formal economy producing DIY equipment and materials.) Overall, however, we do not believe that in recent years the self-service economy (including housework, DIY and other activities) has grown much faster than the formal economy.

Whether the black economy has grown in recent years is doubtful. *Schwarzarbeit* appears to be above all a second job activity, and the unemployed face greater disadvantages than those in employment in seeking moonlighting opportunities. The depressed state of the economy in recent years will have cut both ways; on the one hand more people may have been seeking work in the black economy to augment formal economy incomes or benefit payments; on the other hand, there is no reason to believe that the demand for black economy workers will have been immune to the influence of the cyclical factors which have affected the rest of the labour market. Especially in construction, the depressed level of new house-building will have reduced the demand for 'black' labour. *Schwarzarbeit* in repair businesses and 'off-the-books' trading in general may, however, be increasing, due to rises in VAT and gross labour costs.

5 The Shadow Economy in Britain

As in the previous chapter, the analysis of the shadow economy in Britain is broken down into an analysis of the size of the black economy (ie concealed market economy transactions), and of the size of the self-service economy (non-market productive activity, which is generally not included in the official national accounts statistics).

The size of the black economy

The legislation prohibiting *Schwarzarbeit* ('black work') in Germany has no counterpart in the UK. Moonlighting and 'off-the-books' trading are illegal in the UK only insofar as they involve tax evasion; there is no general prohibition on informal or unlicensed trading arrangements, over and above the specific tax legislation.

This difference between Britain and Germany has two consequences. Firstly, one empirical question, the extent to which business is carried on in contravention of the laws prohibiting *Schwarzarbeit* has no counterpart in the UK. The only relevant question in the UK is the extent to which economic activity in the UK is accompanied by tax evasion, and the investigation is most usefully organised according to the areas where scope for tax evasion arises.

The second consequence of the lack of a law prohibiting *Schwarzarbeit* in the UK is that customer accounts of the black economy in the UK might be expected to be more reliable than in Germany. The German law prohibiting *Schwarzarbeit* puts both the customer and the supplier in the black economy on the wrong side of the law; by contrast, failing to declare sales or income for tax in the UK usually involves only the supplier in any illegal action. Apart from a possible desire to protect their supplier of black economy goods and services, one would expect customers in the UK black economy to have little motive for concealing their 'black' purchases from statisticians and economic researchers.

As in Germany, deduction of employees' income tax at source eliminates most of the scope for tax evasion on employee income. Greater scope for tax evasion arises on earnings from second jobs and casual incomes not covered by PAYE, and on self-employment incomes. These two areas have formed the principal focus of this investigation into tax evasion in the UK. In addition to the separate analysis of second jobholders and the self employed in the next two sections, the UK work has also considered the scope for global, 'macroeconomic', estimates of the scale of incomes not declared for tax, based on analysis of income expenditure differences and other national accounts discrepancies.

Concealed second job holding

As in the German analysis in the last chapter, the topic of concealed incomes from second jobs has to be approached using information on second jobs in general, including both second jobs on which tax is being paid as well as second jobs on which tax is being evaded.

The scope for tax evasion on earnings from second jobs arises for two reasons. About one-third of second jobs are held in a self-employed capacity (General Household Survey, 1981 p85), compared to only about one in ten main jobs. Self-employed second job holders experience the scope for evasion provided by self-employment in general — having control over the reporting of income to the Inland Revenue, and over tax payments. In addition, second job earnings from employment will often be sufficiently low to fall below the PAYE threshold (currently £38.50 per week), and will therefore not be taxed automatically at source. While the Inland Revenue nonetheless obtain from employers details of names, addresses and wages paid to employees earning below the PAYE threshold and do try to match this information to the subsequent tax returns of the employees involved, this procedure is clearly less infallible than PAYE deduction at source, and greater scope for evasion exists.

Second job holding in the UK has been studied by Alden (1981) and Brown, Levin, Rosa and Ulph (1984), using information from a variety of statistical sources. There were considerable differences in the rates of second job holding in different surveys. Brown et al reported that estimates of second job activity rates ranged from 3 per cent to 12 per cent in three different surveys in 1971, and there was a wide range in the results for more recent years too. Part of the variation in the answers seems due to the time horizon of the question asked. Thus, the 1981 General Household Survey found that 4 per cent of job holders reported having a second job 'last week', but 7 per cent of job holders reported that they had a second job when no time frame was specified. It would appear, therefore, that a high percentage of second jobs are held only intermittently.

But an additional source of difference has been suggested by Brown et al. They noted that in a 1971 survey by the Social Science Research Council, which asked a number of questions about second jobs, the response rate declined as the questions became more specific, and began to touch on the subjects of payment and taxation. It would appear that the format of the survey interview and the way the questions are asked could affect the results obtained; perhaps people with second job incomes that they are not declaring for tax may be less inclined to reveal their second jobs to some surveys. One might indeed suspect that some second job moon-lighters would not respond honestly to any survey, in which case the level of second job holding might be understated throughout.

Second jobs are most likely to be held by people unable to vary the total hours worked in their main job. Main job overtime rates will generally be more advantageous than second job earnings. It might be predicted that reductions in the working week would have encouraged more people to seek second jobs, but in fact the evidence suggests that there is no straightforward relationship between the number of hours people work in their main job and the likelihood of them taking a second job. (This seems also to be true in Germany.) Analysis of Family Expenditure Survey data for 1982 shows that the percentage of men holding second jobs tends, if anything, to rise as the number of hours worked in the main job rises. Female second job holders, however, tend to be more common amongst those working fewer hours in their main job. (Smith, 1986, Table 6.3).

A lot of second job holding is by professional workers in public administration and business people whose main jobs afford little scope for flexibility in the hours worked, and who may have skills that they can make use of in second jobs. (Table 5.1) By contrast, people in occupations where overtime is often available (eg manufacturing, construction) are less likely to have second jobs.

Overall, about one third of second jobs are in the same kind of occupation as the person's main job. A lot of second jobs involve low skill and are poorly paid. About 10 per cent of second jobs held

Table 5.1   Who are the second job holders?

Occupation group of main job	% holding a second job	
	Men	Women
Professional and related supporting management in education, welfare and health	10	5
Literary, artistic and sports	11	1
Other professional and managerial	3	3
Clerical and related	4	4
Selling	4	2
Security and protective service	2	1
Catering, cleaning, hairdressing and other personal services	3	4
Farming, fishing and related	4	5
Manufacturing, repairing, etc	2	2
Construction, mining	2	0
Other	3	4
ALL OCCUPATIONS	3	4

Source: General Household Survey 1981

by men are in security occupations, about one fifth of women's second jobs involve selling, and over two fifths are in catering, cleaning, hairdressing and other personal services.

Even if many people holding second jobs do not declare their earnings from such jobs for tax, the tax losses are unlikely to be great in relation to the total income tax yield. Second jobs are held by only a proportion of the population, generally for only a few hours a week, and some may be quite poorly paid. Brown et al (1984) estimate that total income earned in second jobs was only about 0.8 per cent of total income earned in main jobs. Even if tax were evaded on two-thirds of this income the amount of tax lost from second job tax evasion would amount to only about 1 per cent of Inland Revenue income tax receipts, and the level of factor incomes concealed due to tax evasion would amount to less than 0.4 per cent of GDP.

Self-employment incomes

The prolonged recession since 1979 has been accompanied by a sharp rise in the number of people self-employed in Britain, from 1.84 million in 1979 to 2.2 million in 1983, a rise of almost 20 per cent. This rise took place when total employment was falling, and implied an even sharper rise in the percentage of the employed workforce who were self-employed, from 7.5 per cent in 1979 to 9.5 per cent in 1983. The rise in self-employment has occured in all parts of industry, but has been particularly marked in the construction industry.

A number of factors may account for the recent revival of self-employment after a long period of decline. Incentives on the 'supply side' could account for some part of the rise — for example redundant workers setting up in business on their own account. These incentives may have been strengthened by government measures to encourage unemployed workers to set up in business. Allen and Hunn (1985) estimate that about half the 50,000 workers currently receiving financial benefits under the Enterprise Allowance Scheme, introduced in 1983, would not have set up in business without the allowance. More generally, self-employment may have benefited from the development of a climate in which 'enterprise' is encouraged, and the tax and administrative burdens on small business lessened.

Some further part of the rise in self-employment may reflect changes in either technology or management practice, leading to the subcontracting of certain services formerly performed 'in house'. Subcontracting of specialist services permits greater flexibility in their use, and reduces overheads. There seems to be an increasing tendency to subcontract activities such as computer services, marketing and public relations, and even design and tool room functions in some engineering companies.

Whilst there may be good reasons for the rise in self-employment, and the economy may benefit from greater enterpreneurial activity and more efficient use of specialist services, the rise in self-employment clearly does increase the problems of tax collection. Two aspects may be particularly important — the implications for VAT collection, and the implications for income tax collection.

In the case of VAT collection, it is possible to be reasonably sanguine about certain aspects of the rise in self-employment. Some of the smallest new businesses will for some time have a level of turnover below the VAT registration limit (at present £19,500 annual turnover). In addition, companies supplying services to other business firms may gain little competitive advantage from evading VAT, since most of their business customers will be able to recover VAT paid on inputs anyway. Off-the-books trading (keeping a certain proportion of turnover hidden from the sight of the VAT man) is most likely to be a problem with companies selling high-value-added services to private householders — construction and personal services for example.

Income tax evasion may often go hand-in-hand with off-the-books income items, although a further source of income tax evasion involves overstating business expenses — perhaps by fraudulently charging certain items of personal expenditure to the business. There seems considerable evidence that in one way or another self-employed taxpayers in the UK are able to evade a considerable portion of the income tax due. The Central Statistical Office's estimates of national income include a substantial adjustment for incomes from self-employment not reported to the Inland Revenue. This estimated component, which is based in part on the views of the Inland Revenue about the level of unreported self-employment income, amounted to some one seventh of total self-employment income in 1980-82.

Similar conclusions are reached by the analysis of self-employment consumption patterns undertaken as part of this project by

Stephen Smith, Chris Pissarides and Guglielmo Weber, and reported in Smith (1986). The notion that a comparison of the consumption patterns of self-employed and employee households might provide some clue to the levels of concealed self-employment income was first explored by O'Higgins (1981), using published Family Expenditure Survey data to compare aggregate income: expenditure ratios for employee and self-employed households in different income bands. The Smith/Pissarides/Weber analysis was based on household income and expenditure data in the 1982 Family Expenditure Survey, and analysed households' spending on particular groups of commodities in relation to declared household income.

The hypothesis underlying the research was that the self-employed have a much greater opportunity for concealing income from the tax authorities, and that this would be evident from a comparison of their spending patterns with those of employees. At the same levels of reported income, for example, the self-employed may spend more on particular goods than otherwise similar employees do. Their more 'affluent' consumption pattern may give sufficient information to enable an estimate to be made of the 'true' incomes of the self-employed, and hence of the amount of income concealed by the self-employed.

The approach was based on the estimation of relationships between reported income levels and expenditure on particular goods. Three examples, for spending on three groups of purchases by 'blue-collar' households, are shown in Table 5.2. These relationships show that households with higher incomes have, on average, a higher level of spending on the three groups of commodities. Spending is also affected by a range of other factors not shown in the table, but included in the estimated equations: the number of adults and children in the household, the age of the head of the household, the type of housing tenure, and the season of the year can affect the level and pattern of household spending.

The first three equations in Table 5.2 include a dummy variable for self-employed households. In two of the three equations this is statistically significant at the 5 per cent level, indicating significant differences between employee households and self-employed households in the relationship between income and expenditure. The estimates of income under-reporting by the self-employed are based on the second group of three equations where both the

Table 5.2   Consumption equations, 1982, for 'blue collar' households

Equation number	Dependent variable: In(expenditure) on:	Constant	Self-employed (SE)	Ln(net income) (Y)	Y*SE	$\bar{R}^2$
1	Food, drink, and tobacco	0.66 (6.7)*	0.089 (3.5)*	0.30 (17.7)*		0.50
2	Pre-commitments	0.83 (6.9)*	0.085 (2.7)*	0.25 (11.9)*		0.58
3	Other non-durables	0.21 (1.5)	0.040 (1.1)	0.53 (22.8)*		0.40
4	Food, drink, and tobacco	0.66 (6.7)*	-0.002 (0.01)	0.30 (17.1)*	0.021 (0.4)	0.50
5	Pre-commitments	0.81 (6.7)*	0.41 (1.6)	0.25 (11.8)*	-0.076 (1.2)	0.58
6	Other non-durables	0.22 (1.6)	-0.24 (0.8)	0.53 (22.0)*	0.065 (1.0)	0.40

Notes: In addition, each equation included variables representing the age (and age^2) of the head of household, the number of adults, children and tax units in the household, dummy variables for council and private tenants, mortgage payments, and region, and seasonal dummies. The coefficients on these variables are not reported here for reasons of space, but further details are available on request from the authors. t-statistics are shown in parentheses below the coefficients; an asterisk shows coefficients significant at the 5 per cent level.

intercept and the marginal property to consume out of reported income are allowed to differ between employee and self-employed households. At average income these three equations show self-employed households spending 8.9 per cent, 8.5 per cent and 4.0 per cent more than employee households, implying that the income of self-employed households is understated by 30 per cent, 34 per cent and 8 per cent respectively.

Smith (1986) reports a greater range of results, for white collar households as well as blue collar households. Across all the equations, self-employment incomes appear understated, in relation to employee incomes, by 18 per cent. Across all the equations where there are statistically significant differences between employee and self-employed households' consumption patterns, the level of self-employed incomes appears understated by 32 per cent. Some ten percentage points or so of these differences may reflect differences in the periods to which the income data in the Family Expenditure Survey refer (the income from employment figures are current, but the income from self-employment figures refer to some months previous). Overall, therefore, these estimates would suggest that self-employment incomes may be underrecorded in the Family Expenditure Survey by between 10 and 20 per cent. A level of concealed self-employment income within this range would be broadly consistent with the adjustments for evasion that are made in calculating total self-employment income in the national accounts.

The interpretation of national accounts discrepancies

The approach to estimating the scale of incomes concealed by the self-employed which was outlined in the previous section rests on the assumption that some survey data is correct (the expenditure data), whilst other data (the income data) is falsely reported. This assumption may of course be false. Some respondents might realise that an affluent lifestyle would betray their tax evasion, and might adjust their spending records downwards accordingly. Other re-spondents may realise that they have nothing to fear from the confidential Family Expenditure Survey, and may tell the interviewer about income items that they had concealed from the taxman. Both are certainly possibilities, but perhaps the most likely outcome is the one implicitly assumed above, that (at least some) items of expenditure are correctly recorded, while the incomes reported to FES are the same as those reported to the Inland Revenue.

In addition to the possibilities of inaccurate reponse, there are the problems that arise from non-response. Whilst the response rate to the Family Expenditure Survey, about 70 per cent, is remarkably high for such a demanding inquiry, there remains the possibility that the households who respond to the survey are not typical of the population as a whole. Those who choose not to respond may be those with above average black economy earnings. If this were so, conclusions based on reported income: expenditure discrepancies will tend to underestimate the overall level of tax evasion.

The possibility that the veracity of statistical sources may be affected by growth in the black economy has long been recognised. Writers such as Gutmann (1979) and Reuter (1982) have drawn attention to the possibility that macroeconomic statistics, such as Gross Domestic Product, which are used to chart macroeconomic policy may be affected by errors in the underlying data used in their construction.

One aspect of this is reflected in the recognition in official UK statistics that the income data used to calculate the income measure of GDP may be affected by evasion. The income measure is largely based on information from income tax returns, and will thus not reflect incomes on which tax is evaded. The Initial Residual Difference, the gap between the initial measures of GDP based on income and expenditure data, has been as much as 4 per cent of GDP, and an 'evasion adjustment', added to the initial income measure, has been used to bring the income and expenditure measures of GDP more closely into line.

Of course, if the expenditure data is accurate and unaffected by evasion, this process is sufficient to ensure that the resulting GDP statistics are unaffected by the inaccuracy of the income data. The question arises as to what further inaccuracy in the basic data could be tolerated without serious inaccuracies appearing in the GDP estimates. In particular, if people heavily active in the black economy fail to respond to the Family Expenditure Survey, does this mean that the national accounts, which are based in part on the expenditure data from this survey, become suspect?

It will be noted that the comparison between the income and expenditure estimates of GDP does not provide the only opportunity for cross-checking in systems of national accounts. In theory at least a third measure of GDP is possible, based on output statistics, and this could provide a way of cross checking against both the income-based and expenditure-based GDP estimates. In practice, a complete and independent output-based estimate of GDP is not made in the UK, partly because of the lack of output statistics from small firms. Use of the output estimate is largely confined to analysis of changes over time — especially volume changes — and a fully independent output-based estimate of the level of GDP is not available for comparison with the other two measures.

Nonetheless, there are points in the accounts where a growing black economy would be identified. Figure 5.1 shows in schematic form three cross-checking opportunities in the UK national accounts. Two are those already identified: the comparison between the income and expenditure measures of GDP (the initial residual difference), and the microeconomic analysis of income: expenditure discrepancies in survey data, as discussed in the previous section. The third cross-checking opportunity arises in the commodity flow accounts.

The commodity flow accounts are a set of tables that match the supply and demand for some forty different commodity groups, covering the whole economy. They are a form of condensed input output table, in that intermediate demand for each commodity is shown only in total, and not by individual purchasing industry. But they differ from the published UK input output tables in that the discrepancies between supply and demand are shown explicitly, for each commodity.

The tables rest on an accounting identity between 'demand' (reflecting expenditures, including stockbuilding) and 'supply' (output or turnover). At an aggregate level the discrepancy between demand and supply is quite small, averaging less than 1 per cent in the six years 1978 - 83. This in itself proves nothing about the black economy. Both sides of the identity could be affected by the growth of black economy activities. Consumers' expenditure might be understated if black economy operators failed to respond to the Family Expenditure Survey, and if their spending was on average higher than the spending of the people who did respond to the survey. Turnover might be understated if 'off-the-books' business by moonlighters and others were not reflected in official turnover statistics.

On the other hand the separate commodity flow tables for each commodity group might be expected to reflect any differential growth in the black economy in different sectors. Thus, for example,

The Shadow Economy in Britain and Germany

Figure 5.1   Income: expenditure discrepancies and the shadow economy

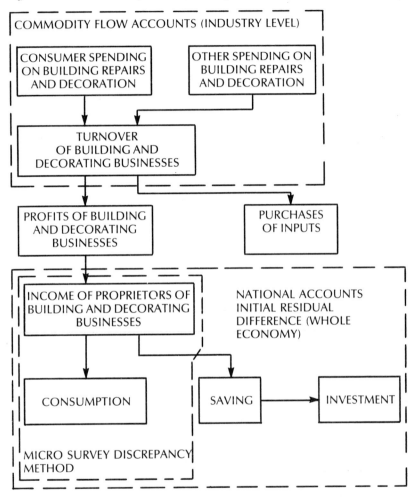

a rise in the black economy in building repairs and decoration would be reflected in an excess of demand over supply in the account for the construction sector, but any corresponding under-statement of consumer's expenditure by black economy builders would be spread across all sectors. Given the concentration of anecdotes about the UK black economy in a limited number of sectors, it is likely that such a pattern of differential growth would be observed. Smith (1986) observes that in two of the sectors where the UK black economy is popularly believed to be large, construction and hotels and catering, the accounts show a significant excess (of about 7 per cent) of demand over supply. But other sectors where there is no reason to expect a large black economy show larger discrepancies, and the discrepancies for construction and hotels and catering are by no means out of line with the apparent level of statistical error in the commodity flow accounts as a whole.

Conclusions from this discussion should be drawn with caution. Nonetheless, it does appear that the problems created for the national accounts by non-response in expenditure surveys can be overstated. Where a growing black economy is concentrated in a limited number of sectors, the commodity flow accounts provide one instrument for detecting its growth. As things stand in the UK, the commodity flow accounts provide little evidence of rapid and substantial growth in the black economy in any sector. Whilst by no means conclusive, this does at least accord reasonably well with the conclusions of the micro-based analyses in earlier sections.

The size of the self-service economy

Under this heading we analyse three areas of productive activity in the self-service economy: housework, DIY and productive activities in clubs and voluntary organisations.

Housework
The amount of time devoted to the production of goods and services within the household economy in the UK is almost as great as the amount of time spent on work in the formal economy. According to a time budget study conducted amongst 450 households in the town of Reading in 1973, the average adult spent about 21 hours per week on work in the household economy compared to 22 hours per week on work in the formal economy. Women who were not employed in the formal economy spent the most time working in the household economy — about forty-two hours per week on domestic work, childcare and shopping. Women who were employed in the formal economy worked on average twenty-five hours in the household economy, in addition to twenty-five hours paid work each week. Men's work was much more heavily concen-

trated in the formal economy — about thirty hours a week paid work compared with only about nine hours household work (Bullock, Dickens, Shapcott and Steadman, 1974).

Comparing these figures to those for Germany in the previous chapter shows a somewhat lower level of time spent on household work by the average household in Britain — some 40 hours per week in Britain compared to 58 hours per week (in 1972) in Germany. (It should of course be noted that there are some differences in the time classifications used, and households in Reading may not be typical of households in Britain.) A higher percentage of household work appears to be done by women in the UK — three quarters in the UK compared to two thirds in Germany. (Note however that the German figures refer to the 1980s, when the amount of household work done by men may have been greater than a decade earlier!) As in Germany, the amount of time spent on housework by working wives is considerably less than the amount of time spent by full time housewives.

The substitutability of household work for formal economy work might be considered in two respects. Firstly, there is the issue of whether differences in the (formal) economic position of households at a given point in time lead to differences in the amount of household work they do. Secondly, there is the issue of substitition over time.

The differences between working women and full time housewives in the amount of housework done does suggest some substitutability between household and formal production. Some of the differences may reflect differences in the circumstances of households where both partners work — there may be no need to cook a midday meal, for example — but, as argued in the last chapter, other differences may reflect more conscious substitution decisions, such as purchases of more expensive convenience foods by the households of working women. Nevertheless, it is clear that the scope for substitution is limited by cultural factors. As Pahl (1984) has found, the employment status of the male partner in the household does not appear to have any marked effect on the balance of responsibility for household tasks. In households where the husband was unemployed the burden of household work was, if anything, borne more heavily by the woman; in these cases there was little evidence that household work was substituted for (unavailable) formal work.

Over time, however, there do appear to have been some important substitutions between formal work and household work. Painstaking work by Gershuny and Thomas (1980) to reconstruct earlier time budget studies on a consistent basis has shown some major changes over the years in the labour time devoted to housework. A summary of this data in Gershuny (1983) shows two interesting phases. Firstly there was a sharp rise of some 70 per cent in the time spent on housework by middle class women between 1937 and 1961. This would appear to reflect a reduction in the amount of domestic work performed by paid labour in middle class households, a process of substitution which must in part have reflected a sharp rise in the cost of employing domestic servants. The second phase, during the 1960s and 1970s, saw a gradual decline in the amount of time spent on housework by both middle class and working class housewives. Gershuny argued that this decline was taking place simultaneously with a rise in the productivity of household labour time, and did not reflect a decline in the output of the household economy. What he believed was happening was that rising formal economy incomes, rather than leading to substitution away from household work (as the cross section of households' housework times in 1937 would have indicated), were instead encouraging wealthier households to maintain, or even increase, their amounts of household production, using new labour saving equipment and materials. As a result household work times were no longer a good measure of household's production of goods and services. Moreover changes in the level and pattern of incomes in the formal economy would no longer provide unambiguous predictions of associated changes in the output of the household economy. Reduced formal economy incomes would reduce the opportunity cost of labour in the household economy, but would also reduce households' abilities to buy the equipment and materials needed for household production.

DIY home repairs and decorations

Commentators such as Pahl (1984) have drawn attention to a substantial growth in the sixties and seventies in the amount of DIY home decorations, improvement and repair work done by householders in the UK. This growth has been accompanied by the development of a specialist DIY retail sector catering for DIY workers, and, more recently, by the growth in large 'DIY superstores' providing a wide range of DIY materials and equipment to retail customers and small businesses.

Whilst there is every reason to believe that substantial growth in the DIY activities of households has taken place, the indications are that growth in the sector has levelled off since the late 1970s. The percentage of respondents to the General Household Survey who said they had done DIY work in the previous month stayed quite constant at between 35 and 37 per cent between 1977 and 1983, and Smith (1986, Table 15.1) presents evidence that there was little change over the same period in the frequency of households' purchases of paint and other DIY materials and equipment.

The highest rates of participation in DIY home decoration and repair work are by people in the 30-44 age group (similar to Germany); there is a much more pronounced peak in DIY participation at this age group than in either of the two other productive leisure activities shown in Table 5.3. DIY work is most common amongst people in professional, managerial and skilled manual occupations, and much less common amongst people in semi-skilled and unskilled manual occupations, and in junior non-manual occupations. Taken on its own, this pattern might suggest that DIY participation was higher amongst groups with a relatively high opportunity cost of time, perhaps a rather surprising conclusion.

However, in fact the occupational background of DIY workers is largely a reflection of the pattern of house ownership amongst people in different occupational groups. Evidence from expenditures on DIY materials (Smith, 1986 Table 15.1) shows twice as many purchases of DIY materials and equipment amongst owner occupiers than amongst council tenants, and three times as many as amongst private tenants.

These differences are likely to reflect two different factors:
(i) differences between owner occupiers, council tenants and private tenants in the responsibility for routine maintenance, repairs and decoration, and
(ii) the ability of owner occupiers to benefit from any appreciation in the capital value of their property, resulting from home improvement work.
It is in these areas that some differences in the pattern and level of DIY activitiy between Britain and Germany might be expected.

In the first place, owner occupation is more common in Britain than in Germany: some 60 per cent of households are owner-

Table 5.3   Productive leisure activities: characteristics of participants

| | Great Britain, 1983 Persons aged 16 and over Percentage participating in the four weeks before survey | | |
	Gardening	DIY	Dressmaking/ needlework/ knitting
Men	50	51	2
Women	39	24	48
All Adults	44	36	27
Age 16-19	16	21	18
Age 20-24	23	35	24
Age 25-29	38	44	27
Age 30-44	52	49	29
Age 45-59	53	41	29
Age 60-69	53	32	30
Age 70 and over	39	16	23
By socio-economic group:			
Professional	61	67	10
Employers and managers	58	51	15
Intermediate non-manual	54	44	39
Junior non-manual	43	31	44
Skilled manual and own- account non-professional	46	45	11
Semi-skilled manual	39	28	30
Unskilled manual	38	23	28

Source: General Household Survey, 1983.

occupiers in Britain compared to 44 per cent in Germany. Moreover, more of the owner-occupied housing stock in Britain consists of older houses (as opposed to newer apartments), where the scope for beneficial DIY improvements may be particularly great.

Amongst tenants, however, the extent of DIY work may be lower than in Germany. Council tenants have traditionally been discouraged from undertaking even trivial repair and maintenance work themselves, although the situation is changing, partly as a result of restrictions on local authority spending. In the private rented sector, 'unfurnished' rental accommodation has been in decline for many years; the most common form of tenancy is 'furnished' accommodation, where the landlord is responsible for maintenance and interior decoration, as well as furnishing.

The General Household Survey does not record information on the amount of time that households spent on DIY work, but only on the number of households doing such work. The data does not, therefore, permit an estimate of the value of DIY work calculated on the same basis as in Germany, by valuing time inputs. In any event, as was remarked earlier, the low productivity of DIY workers makes a time valuation approach particularly unreliable. An alternative, which might provide a better comparison between DIY output and the output of builders and decorators in the formal economy, would be to proceed from households' purchases of DIY materials and equipment, and then to estimate the 'value added' by DIY workers by applying the ratio of materials purchased to value added by builders and decorators in the formal economy.

In 1983 the average annual expenditure on materials and equipment for DIY home repairs, maintenance and decoration by households in Britain was £121, compared to £49 on payments to contractors. The ratio of materials purchased to gross value added in firms doing building completion work (Group 504: painting and decorating, plastering etc) was 1:1.45 in 1981 (Business Monitor PA500). Assuming this ratio to have been unchanged between 1981 and 1983 would imply total value added by DIY workers of some £3.7 billion in 1983, equivalent to some 1.4 per cent of GDP.

Activities in clubs and voluntary organisations

Compared to Germany, Britain has less of a tradition of social organisation in clubs and societies. Nonetheless, a wide range of voluntary work is done, through a variety of formal and less formal institutions, and it does not appear that the percentage of the population doing such work is any less in Britain than in Germany.

Indeed, Table 5.4 shows a very high participation rate in voluntary work in Britain. Almost a quarter of adults interviewed by the 1981 General Household Survey said that in the twelve months before the interview they had done some voluntary work — that is, work for which they were not paid, which was of service to others apart from their immediate family and friends. Examples of the work done included raising money for a good cause, organising youth clubs and playgroups, helping the sick and handicapped, voluntary public

Table 5.4   Participation in voluntary work, Great Britain, 1981

	% of persons aged 16 and over
All adults	23
Men	21
Women	24
Age: 16-24	18
25-34	24
35-44	30
45-64	24
65+	17
Dependent children in household	27
No children in household	20
Working full-time	23
Working part-time	29
Economically inactive	20
Full-time students	32
Unemployed	16

Source: General Household Survey, 1981 Tables 8.1, 8.4, 8.8

service (eg as a school governor), working for community groups and pressure groups, etc. The survey found that women did voluntary work more often than men (24% of women, as against 21% of men), and the proportion doing voluntary work varied with age, falling after a peak of 30% of those in the 35 - 44 age group to 17% of those over 65.

The survey found a strong association between the likelihood of people doing voluntary work and their social and economic status. People in professional occupations were more than three times as likely to do voluntary work as unskilled manual workers. It is noteworthy that the type of voluntary work done mirrored to a considerable extent the occupation and social status of the volunteers. (Table 5.5)

People who apparently had the most time to spare did not appear more inclined to do voluntary work. Indeed, groups which might be expected to have more time available, such as people without

Table 5.5   Volunteers and the voluntary work they do

Socio-economic group of volunteer	TYPE OF VOLUNTARY ACTIVITY								
	Raising money	Com-mittee work	Teach-ing and coaching	Giving advice	Holidays and enter-tain-ments	Practical help to indivi-duals	Help at play groups	Help at youth clubs	Other practical work
Professional	39	42	11	15	14	26	3	8	22
Employers and managers	46	36	11	9	9	27	4	7	18
Intermediate and junior non-manual	40	26	12	7	11	27	4	10	16
Skilled manual and self employed non-professional	37	21	8	4	8	33	4	6	14
Semi-skilled manual and personal service	42	14	8	3	9	35	4	4	17
Unskilled manual	37	14	4	2	9	48	2	3	21
All volunteers	41	26	10	7	10	30	4	7	17

Source: General Household Survey 1981, Table 8.21

children and the unemployed, showed lower than average participation rates in voluntary work.

It is clear that the patterns noted in the preceding two paragraphs are not consistent with a simple 'opportunity cost' model of participation in voluntary work. Such a model might suggest that if voluntary work yielded rewards that were a substitute for work in the formal economy, voluntary work participation would be greater amongst those with spare time and low earning potential in the formal economy. Clearly the matter is more complex than this, and the predictions that might be derived from the opportunity cost model — for example, that voluntary work may have risen in recent years in response to high unemployment and reductions in the working week — should be viewed with some scepticism.

6 Conclusions : effects and policy implications

In this chapter we summarise our conclusions about the size of the shadow economy in Britain and Germany. We then go on to consider the effects of the shadow economy; in what ways does the shadow economy interact with the formal economy, and does this interaction have desirable or undesirable consequences? Finally, we consider the implications for economic policy. In particular, two issues come to the fore. Firstly, would economic policymakers be better served by a new system of national accounts, which attempted to reflect activities in the shadow economy as well as those in the formal economy? Secondly, in what ways should economic policy seek to control the shadow economy; specifically, what kinds of tax and tax enforcement policies should be pursued?

The size of the shadow economy

The 'shadow economy', which has been the subject of the two research projects reported here, covers a wide range of productive economic activity. What the activities in the shadow economy have in common is that they may be poorly reflected in the national accounts statistics of Gross Domestic Product, national income, etc. Where they differ is in the reasons for this.

Some of the productive activity in the shadow economy ought to be included in the national accounts, but may be missing because the attempts to conceal moonlighting and other tax evasion mislead the statisticians as well as the taxman. These activities — the so-called 'black economy' — are the part of the shadow economy which has achieved the greatest public attention. Some staggering estimates have been made of how big the black economy might be. Our researches suggest that in overall terms it is in fact quite modest — though in some particular activities it may be much larger. The estimate from the Institute for Fiscal Studies for the size of the black economy in Britain is between 3 and 5 per cent of Gross Domestic Product; the Tübingen researchers put the German figure at a maximum of 5 per cent of GDP. These estimates suggest that the problem of the black economy may be of similar dimensions in each country; but the methods of quantification used are by no means accurate enough nor sufficiently comparable to make any more precise comparison.

A much greater area of shadow economy activity is missing from the national accounts by definition. This is the legal, but non-monetary 'self-service' economy, including both unpaid housework and DIY, and also the unpaid work that people do through clubs and voluntary organisations. In both countries the national accounts are largely restricted to production which can be given a straightforward monetary valuation, and so very little of the self-service economy is included. Both in Britain and Germany this part of the shadow economy is quantitatively much more important than the illegal black economy; indeed, on average, people spend scarcely less time doing unpaid work such as bringing up children, household chores, shopping, cooking, decorating, gardening and the like than they spend on formal paid jobs. Measuring the value of the output produced by the self-service economy is possible only with the aid of very debatable assumptions, but the massive importance of these activities is evident.

Has either part of the shadow economy grown in importance in recent years? The methods for quantifying the black economy could not be expected to reveal anything apart from the most substantial changes in its economic importance, and certainly neither project found any evidence that it had grown — or declined — markedly in the last five or ten years. Over the longer term, there have in the post-war period been conflicting influences on the level of black economy activities. The rise in taxation may have provided some encouragement to the black economy — particularly when major changes were introduced, such as the imposition of value added tax on services in the UK in 1973, and the replacement of the turnover tax by value added tax in Germany in 1968. On the other hand, the growing concentration of economic activity amongst larger firms, and the development of improved methods of financial control using computers, electronic cash registers, etc will have worked in the opposite direction. The black economy is now likely to be largely confined to people working on their own account and to smaller firms supplying high value added services to private households — but in some such areas it may be very significant.

What about the self-service economy? Some have suggested (eg Rose, 1983) that the self-service economy provides an opportunity for people to offset some of the effects of a recession in the formal economy : as opportunities for work in the formal economy decline, people produce more in the domestic economy. On this view, the poor condition of the formal economy in the late 1970s and early 1980s might have been (partly) counterbalanced by a rise in self-service production. The evidence does not appear to support such a view, however. The time spent on household work has been in gradual decline over a number of years. The development of labour-saving equipment and materials has increased the productivity of household work, with the result that the fall in housework times may not necessarily imply a fall in the output of the household economy. Nevertheless, it is precisely this increased dependence on expensive capital equipment which constrains the ability of the unemployed and those with falling formal economy incomes to increase their household production. DIY home improvements, for example, require both time to do the work, and money for materials. Recession in the formal economy may increase the availability of time, at the same time reducing the financial means necessary to participate effectively in the self-service economy.

The effects of the shadow economy

An analysis of the 'effects' of the shadow economy requires an explicit yardstick for comparison. This yardstick needs to be a feasible alternative situation; one that could exist, if conditions were different in certain specific respects. Thus, for example, it does not make sense to talk about the 'effects' of the household economy in total, because it is not clear how to conceive of a situation where no household production took place at all. On the other hand, it does make sense to consider the consequences of small marginal changes in household production, and in particular to consider substitution at the margin between formal production, and production in the shadow economy.

Such a process of substitution might be influenced by any of the range of possible causes of the shadow economy that we considered in Chapter 2. At one extreme the substitution might reflect purely economic factors, such as the level of taxation on production in the formal economy. At the other extreme, the substitution might be a response to non-economic factors — the greater satisfaction from working for oneself, for example.

Many of the characteristics of the process of substitution between the formal and shadow economies are the same for both substitution towards the black economy, and towards the self-service economy. Consider, for example, substitution between painting and decorating in the formal economy, similar activities in the black economy, and DIY painting and decorating. In each case, the choice of shadow economy production rather than production in the formal economy results in a reduction in the level of tax revenues accruing to the state, and a lower level of social insurance receipts (unemployment, accident and health insurance, etc contributions in Germany, National Insurance in the UK).

The effects on economic welfare are in both cases more complex. Production in the shadow economy is not unambiguously a 'bad thing'; some of the work done in the black economy or as DIY might not be done if it were subject to the levels of taxation ruling in the formal economy, and both the black economy and DIY may provide greater scope for creativity and enterprise than the formal economy. But on the other hand there is a risk that some of the work in the black economy, or done as DIY, may be done less efficiently than it would be in the formal economy. Efficient firms may be undercut by their less efficient rivals in the black economy, and the overall productive efficiency of the economy may be reduced as a result. Equally, the efficiency of the economy is worsened by people choosing to do DIY work if, in the absence of the tax saving through DIY, they would have chosen instead to employ a more efficient producer in the formal economy.

Do we need a new national accounts?

As we have shown, the national accounts of both Britain and Germany do not take account of a large amount of productive activity. Statistics such as GDP may not reflect the true level of economic activity associated with tax evasion. In addition, the vast area of the self service economy is largely omitted from the accounts, by definition. By and large, GDP statistics in both countries concentrate on monetary transactions alone.

These omissions, it has been suggested, may have two consequences. In the first place, it is clear that GDP will not be a good indicator of differences in the standard of living between countries at different stages of development. In less developed countries the household economy tends to be larger relative to the formal economy than in most advanced countries. Comparing relative standards of living by comparing the levels of formal GDP may exaggerate the differences between less developed and industrialised countries. This criticism of GDP is undoubtedly valid. Comparisons of relative standards of living between countries at different stages of development would require a broader indicator than GDP. Nevertheless, the primary purpose of the national accounts statistics is to provide an indicator of short-term changes within an economy, as an aid to macroeconomic management. For this purpose, an extension of GDP statistics to cover non-monetary transactions in the household economy would appear unnecessary, given the large measure of stability which we have found in the borderline between the shadow economy and the formal economy. It could even be confusing, since the extended output indicator, including the self-service economy, would have to depend heavily on assumptions about rather uncertain magnitudes.

A more serious issue about the shadow economy and GDP is the possible way that the black economy might interfere with the signals that GDP gives about the state of the macroeconomy. Growth in the black economy at the expense of the formal economy would show up as a decline in GDP. Policy-makers might be misled by the fall in GDP into trying to stimulate the economy out of a non-existent recession. Mistaken macroeconomic policies may have been pursued as a result of statistical 'illusions'.

Again, our researches suggest that this theoretical possibility has not been a serious problem in practice over the last decade. The

91

black economy is neither large enough, nor is the borderline between the black economy and the formal economy volatile enough, for GDP to have been a misleading indicator of macro-economic performance in either country. The black economy may indeed raise questions about the accuracy and reliability of national accounts statistics, but at present these problems are not significant cause for concern.

How should we control the shadow economy?

Issues of tax policy and tax enforcement arise most obviously in the context of the black economy. However, as we have seen, the level and pattern of taxation may be one of the factors influencing the development of certain aspects of the wider shadow economy — most notably, perhaps, DIY house repairs and decoration, and vehicle servicing. Ideally, one might wish to design a structure of taxation which did not encourage people to choose methods of production which involve higher resource cost, simply because they were taxed less heavily. Unfortunately, that is often precisely what happens when people choose producers in the black economy, or DIY work, in preference to producers in the formal economy. Inefficient producers (or self-service) may be chosen, simply because of the saving of tax.

Devising a 'neutral' tax system in areas where there is considerable substitutability between the formal economy, the black economy and DIY inevitably involves accepting a second best solution. Full enforcement of taxes in the black economy is unlikely to be ever an attainable policy goal, and it is still less likely that a way could be found to levy income tax on self-service labour inputs to DIY. Nevertheless, some possible offset to the tax advantages of the black economy or DIY might be found in the taxation of identifiable inputs to shadow economy production. A higher rate of value-added tax on paint and rolls of wallpaper than on the bills for work done by professional painters and decorators might, for example, go some way towards diminishing the purely tax-related advantages of the shadow economy and DIY production.

Whilst these considerations might provide some guidance as to the appropriate development of tax policy in relation to the shadow economy in general, the more immediate issues in both countries concern the control of the black economy. There are important questions about the level of resources that should be devoted to collecting taxes from the black economy, and about what other measures should be used to control the growth of the sector.

Both countries tend to rely on efficient investigation rather than the level of penalties to control tax evasion. This is particularly marked in the UK, where income tax offences seldom result in prosecution, and more often in low-key agreements to recover the lost tax, sometimes with the addition of surcharges. In Germany also, whilst prosecution is more frequent, its deterrent effect is limited by the low level of the penalties imposed by the courts. The criteria used to determine the level of resources devoted to tax enforcement have not been made explicit in either country. From an economic standpoint however, it is clear that they should reflect the costs of raising revenue alternatively from other sources (the 'marginal cost of public funds'), and the effectiveness of enforcement in ensuring compliance in future periods.

The major contrast in policy towards the black economy in Britain and Germany is the specific legislation in Germany prohibiting *Schwarzarbeit*. This has no counterpart in the UK, where the control of the black economy is limited to the efforts devoted to tax enforcement. It might be wondered whether there would be anything to be gained from enacting specific legislation along the German lines in the UK.

The legislation prohibiting *Schwarzarbeit* in Germany recognises that the problems of the black economy are not purely problems of taxation. Much more than in the UK, the debate on *Schwarzarbeit* in Germany centres on its role in reducing employment opportunities for workers in the formal economy, in damaging the social insurance system, and in weakening the effectiveness of formal apprenticeship and training schemes. In the absence of a similar formal pattern of qualification and employment registration in the UK, particularly in some of the trades where the black economy seems particularly important, it may be difficult to transfer these aspects of the German legislation to the UK situation.

On the other hand, a second aspect of the German legislation may well have lessons for the UK. By making customers who knowingly engage *Schwarzarbeiter* guilty of a crime, the German law reduces the incentive to purchase from the black economy. In the UK, by contrast, there is no such legislation and the law merely requires the seller of services, or the recipient of income, to make the appropriate declaration for tax; the customer of black economy goods and services is unlikely to have broken any law. Often of course, as the German legislation recognises, it may be difficult for the customer to distinguish black economy traders from legitimate ones, and in such instances it would be undesirable to make the customer liable to prosecution. On the other hand, consideration might be given to introducing similar legislation along the German lines, making it an offence knowingly to facilitate tax evasion, or to engage black economy labour. Such a move would, of course, be unlikely to eliminate the black economy entirely, since there would still be scope for mutual financial gain from concealment, and there would be considerable practical problems in enforcing a law of this sort. But by putting the customers of black economy services on the wrong side of the law it would increase the risks they bear, and so might occasionally help to tip the balance in favour of formal economy suppliers.

In general, we believe the black economy to be more of a problem in a moral sense than in its economic impact. We do not think that the problem of unemployment could be solved by trying to eliminate the black economy. Neither would this necessarily improve the financial situation of government or of the social insurance systems. Much of the work done in the black economy (especially in home repairs and decorations) might be done as DIY instead — or indeed not at all — rather than at the higher prices of the formal economy.

There are however sectors where the black economy is not a negligible problem. It is important that governments continue their efforts to control these sectors — and especially any extension of the areas of the economy where firms largely operate in the black economy — not merely to recover the lost revenue, but also to ensure that the moral climate for taxpaying is maintained, and that it is not weakened either by a growing acceptance of tax evasion as innocent entertainment, or by growing resentment on the part of honest taxpayers.

Bibliography

Aberle, H.-J. and Eggenberger, E., 'Die Problematik der Schwarzarbeit aus wirtschaftlicher Sicht', *Wirtschaft und Verwaltung*, 1979, pp193-256.

Arbeitsgemeinschaft Rundfunkwerbung (Editors), *Teleskopie-Strukturerhebungen 1981/82*, various issues, 1983.

Alden, J., 'Holding two jobs: an examination of "moonlighting"', pp43-57, in Henry, S. (ed), *Can I Have It In Cash?*, London, Astragal Books 1981.

Allen, D. and Hunn, A., 'An evaluation of the Enterprise Allowance Scheme', *Employment Gazette*, Vol 93, no 8, pp313-317, August 1985.

Bank of England, 'Recent changes in the use of cash', *Bank of England Quarterly Bulletin*, Vol 22, no 4, pp519-29, 1984.

Becker, G. S., 'A theory of the allocation of time', *Economic Journal*, September 1965.

Blades, D., *The Hidden Economy and the National Accounts*, OECD Economic Outlook, Occasional Studies, Paris, OECD, 1982.

Brown, C. V., Levin, E. J., Rosa, P. J., and Ulph, D. T., 'Tax evasion and avoidance on earned income: some survey evidence', *Fiscal Studies*, Vol 5, No 3, pp1-22, 1984.

The Shadow Economy in Britain and Germany

Bullock, N., Dickens, P., Shapcott, M., and Steadman, P., 'Time budgets and models of urban activity patterns', *Social Trends*, No 5, pp45-63, 1974.

Buttler, G., 'Schattenwirtschaft: Grenzen der Erfaßbarkeit', *Beiträge zur Wirtschafts- und Sozialpolitik aus dem Institut der Deutschen Wirtschaft*, Vol 120/121, Köln 1983.

Cassel, D., 'Schattenwirtschaft — eine Wachstumsbranche?', *List-Forum*, Vol 11, pp343-363, 1982.

Cassel, D. and Caspers, A., 'Was ist Schattenwirtschaft?' *Wirtschaftswissenschaftliches Studium*, Vol 13, pp 1-7, 1984.

Central Statistical Office, 'United Kingdom national accounts: sources and methods', Third edition, *Studies in Official Statistics* No 37, London, HMSO 1985.

Clark, C., 'The economics of housework', *Bulletin of the Oxford Institute of Statistics*, pp205-11, May 1958.

Contini, B., 'The Second Economy of Italy', *Taxing & Spending*, No 3, pp17-24, 1981.

Cowell, F. A., 'The economics of tax evasion: a survey', Economic and Social Research Council Programme on Taxation, Incentives and the Distribution of Income, Discussion Paper No 80, July 1985.

Darkow, M., 'Weitere Bemerkungen zum Tagesablauf 1974/80 und zu Freizeitaktivitäten 1980', pp201-237 in Berg, K. and Kiefer, M.-L. (eds), *Massenkommunikation II, Eine Langzeitstudie zur Mediennutzung und Medienbewertung*, Frankfurt 1982.

Deutscher Bundestag (eds), *Fünfter Bericht der Bundesregierung über Erfahrungen bei der Anwendung des Arbeitnehmerüberlassungsgesetzes — AüG — sowie über die Auswirkungen des Gesetzes zur Bekämpfung der illegalen Beschäftigung — BG* Bundestagsdrucksache 10/1934, 31 August 1984.

Dilnot, A. W. and Morris, C. N., 'What do we know about the black economy?', *Fiscal Studies*, Vol 2, No 1, pp58-73, 1981.

Dornach, B. W., *Selbstversorgung. Das vergessene Wirtschaftssystem*, Köln 1982.

Feige, E. L., 'How big is the irregular economy?', *Challenge*, No 22, pp5-13, November/December 1979.

— , 'The UK's unobserved economy: a preliminary assessment', *Journal of Economic Affairs*, Vol 1, No 4, pp205-12, 1981.

— , 'The meaning of the "underground economy" and the full compliance deficit', in Gaertner, W. and Wenig, A., *The Economics of the Shadow Economy: Proceedings of the International Conference on the Economics of the Shadow Economy held at the University of Bielefeld, West Germany, October 10-14, 1983*, Berlin, Springer Verlag 1985.

— , and McGee, R. T., 'Tax revenue losses and the unobserved economy in the UK', *Journal of Economic Affairs*, Vol 2, No 3, pp164-71, 1982.

Ferman, L. A. and Berndt, L. E., 'The irregular economy', pp26-42 in Henry, S. (ed), *Can I Have It In Cash?*, London, Astragal Books 1981.

Freud, D., 'A guide to underground economics', *Financial Times*, p16, 9 April 1979.

Frey, B. S., 'Schattenwirtschaft und Wirtschaftspolitik', *Kredit und Kapital*, Vol 17, pp103-119, 1984.

— , and Pommerehne, W. W., 'Measuring the Hidden Economy: Though this be madness there is method in it', pp3-27 in Tanzi, V. (ed), *The Underground Economy in the United States and Abroad*, Massachusetts, Lexington 1982.

— , and Pommerehne, W. W., 'Quantitative Erfassung der Schattenwirtschaft: Methoden und Ergebnisse' pp265-293 in Hansmeyer, K.-H. (ed), *Staatsfinanzen im Wandel*, Schriften des Vereins für Sozialpolitik, N. F., Vol 154, Berlin, München 1983.

The Shadow Economy in Britain and Germany

— , and Weck-Hannemann, H., 'The Hidden Economy as an Unobserved Variable', *European Economic Review*, Vol 26, pp33-53, 1984.

— , and Weck-Hannemann, H., 'Measuring the Shadow Economy: The Case of Switzerland.' pp76-104 in Gaertner, W. and Wenig, A., *The Economics of the Shadow Economy*, Springer Verlag, Berlin, 1985.

Gerard, D., *Charities in Britain: Conservatism or Change?*, London, Bedford Square Press 1983.

Gershuny, J. I., *Social Innovation and the Division of Labour*, Oxford University Press 1983.

— , and Pahl, R. E., 'Work outside employment: some preliminary speculations', *New Universities Quarterly*, Vol 34, No 1, pp120-5, 1979. Reprinted in Henry, S. (ed), *Can I Have It In Cash?*, London, Astragal Books 1981.

Gmelin, H., 'Vereine, Gesellschaft, Weiterbildung', pp215-221 im Kongreß der Landesregierung Baden-Württemberg: *Zukunftschancen eines Industrielandes — Herausforderung Weiterbildung*, Staatsministerium Baden-Württemberg, 17-18 December 1984.

Grass, R.-D., *Ausweichwirtschaft*, Frankfurt 1984.

Gruner und Jahr AG & Co. (eds), *Branchenbild Do-it-yourself-Werkzeuge*, 1983.

Gutmann, P. M., 'The subterranean economy', *Financial Analysts' Journal*, pp26-7,34, November-December 1977.

— , 'Statistical illusions, mistaken policies', *Challenge*, No 22, pp14-17, November/December 1979.

Hamer, G., 'Genauigkeitskontrollen bei der Aufstellung Volkswirtschaftlicher Gesamtrechnungen', *Allgemeines Statistisches Archiv*, Vol 54, p76*ff*, 1970.

Hawrylyshyn, O., 'Towards a definition of non-market activities', *Review of Income and Wealth*, May, pp79-96, 1977.

Hilzenbecher, M., *Die (schattenwirtschaftliche) Wertschöpfung der Hausarbeit — Eine empirische Untersuchung für die Bundesrepublik Deutschland*, unpublished manuscript, 1984.

Institut für Demoskopie Allensbach, *Freizeitarbeit 1974*, Studie im Auftrag der Kommission für wirtschaftlichen und sozialen Wandel, 1975.

Jöreskog, K. G., and Van Thillo, M., *LISREL: A general computer program for estimating a linear structural equation system involving multiple indicators of unobserved variables*, Department of Statistics, University of Uppsala, Research Report 73-5, 1973.

Keith Committee, *Committee on Enforcement Powers of the Revenue Departments*, Report, Vols 1 and 2, Cmnd 8822, London, HMSO 1983.

Keller, B., *Die Zeit als ökonomisches Gut*, Forschungsberichte aus dem Institut für Angewandte Wirtschaftsforschung, Series A, Vol 39, Tübingen, 1984.

Kirchgässner, G., 'Verfahren zur Erfassung der Größe und Entwicklung des Schattensektors', Discussion Paper No 211-82, Institut für Volkswirtschaftslehre und Statistik der Universität Mannheim, 1982.

— , 'Size and development of the West German shadow economy, 1955-1980', *Zeitschrift für die gesamte Staatswissenschaft*, Vol 139, pp197-214, 1983.

Krautwald, H., *Ungelöste Probleme im Rahmen der Umsatzbesteuerung — eine Bestandsaufnahme*, Frankfurt, 1982.

Langfeldt, E., *Ursachen der 'Schattenwirtschaft' und ihre Konsequenzen für die Wirtschafts-, Finanz- und Gesellschaftspolitik*, Report of a research project undertaken for the Federal Ministry for Economics. Kiel, 1983.

— , 'Konsequenzen einer wachsenden Schattenwirtschaft für die geldpolitische Steuerung in der Bundesrepublik Deutschland', pp184-203 in Schäfer, W. (ed), *Schattenökonomie*, Göttingen, 1984.

MacAfee, K., 'A glimpse of the hidden economy in the national accounts', *Economic Trends*, No 316, pp81-7, February 1980.

Marschall, D., *Bekämpfung illegaler Beschäftigung. Schwarzarbeit, illegale Ausländerbeschäftigung und illegale Arbeitnehmerüberlassung*, München 1983.

Matthews, K., 'National income and the black economy', *Economic Affairs*, pp261-7, July 1983.

— , and Rastogi, A., 'Little Mo and the moonlighters: another look at the black economy', Liverpool Research Group in Macroeconomics, *Quarterly Economic Bulletin*, Vol 6, No 2, 1985.

Maurice, R. (ed), *National Accounts Statistics: Sources and Methods*, London, HMSO 1968.

Miller, R., 'Evidence of attitudes to evasion from a sample survey', in Seldon, A. (ed), *Tax Avoision*, London, Institute of Economic Affairs 1979.

O'Higgins, M., *Measuring the Hidden Economy: A Review of Evidence and Methodologies*, Outer Circle Policy Unit 1980.

Ollmann, R., Niessen, H.-J. and Ehling, M., 'Eigen- und Schwarzarbeit in der Bundesrepublik', *Wirtschaftsdienst*, 1985/IV, pp197-201, 1985.

Pahl, R. E., *Divisions of Labour*, Oxford, Basil Blackwell 1984.

Peacock, A. and Shaw, G. K., 'Is tax revenue loss overstated?', *Journal of Economic Affairs*, Vol 2, No 3, pp161-3, 1982.

Petersen, H.-G., 'Size of the Public Sector, Economic Growth, and the Informal Economy: Development Trends in the Federal Republic of Germany', *Review of Income and Wealth*, Vol 28, pp191-215, 1982.

Petry, G. and Wied-Nebbeling, S., *Die Gesamtwirtschaftliche Bedeutung der Schattenwirtschaft*, unpublished report, Tübingen, Institut für Angewandte Wirtschaftsforschung 1986.

Reuter, P., 'The irregular economy and the quality of macro-economic statistics', pp125-43 in Tanzi, V. (ed), *The Underground Economy in the United States and Abroad*, Massachusetts, Lexington 1982.

Rose, R., 'Getting by in three economies: the resources of the official, unofficial and domestic economies', University of Strathclyde, Centre for the Study of Public Policy, *Studies in Public Policy*, No 110, 1983.

Schettkat, R., 'The size of household production: Methodological problems and estimates for the FRG.' Paper prepared for the conference 'The economics of the shadow economy', Bielefeld, 10-14 October 1983, 1984.

Schrage, H., 'Schattenwirtschaft — Abgrenzung, Definition, Methoden der quantitativen Erfassung.' pp11-37 in Schäfer, W., (ed), *Schattenökonomie*, Göttingen, 1984.

Smith, S., *Britain's Shadow Economy*, Clarendon Press, Oxford (1986).

Statistisches Bundesamt (eds), *Konten und Standardtabellen 1981, Fachserie 18 (Volkswirtschaftliche Gesamtrechnungen), Reihe 1*, Stuttgart, Mainz, 1982.

Tanzi, V., 'Underground economy and tax evasion in the United States: estimates and implications', Banca Nazionale del Lavoro, *Quarterly Review*, December 1980.

— , 'A second (and more skeptical) look at the underground economy in the United States', in Tanzi, V. (ed), *The Underground Economy in the United States and Abroad*, Massachusetts, Lexington 1982.

Topham, N., 'A reappraisal and recalculation of the marginal cost of public funds', *Public Finance*, Vol 34, No 3, 1984.

The Shadow Economy in Britain and Germany

Tuchtfeldt, E., 'Die Schattenwirtschaft — ein zweiter Wirtschafts-kreislauf', *Zeitschrift für Wirtschaftspolitik*, Vol 33, No 1, pp13-43, 1984.

US Internal Revenue Service, *Estimates of Income Unreported on Individual Income Tax Returns*, Publication no 1104, Washington DC, Government Printing Office, 1979.

Weck, H., 'Wie groß ist die Schattenwirtschaft?' *Wirtschaftsdienst*, Vol 62, pp392-396, 1982.

Weck-Hannemann, H., 'Weiche Modellierung der Schattenwirt-schaft — Ein internationaler Vergleich', pp167-186 in Gretschmann, K., Heinze, G. and Mettelsiefen, B. (eds), *Schattenwirtschaft*, Göttingen 1984.

Weck, H., Pommerehne, W. and Frey, B. S., *Schattenwirtschaft*, München 1984.

Wild, M. and Zander, E., 'Arbeitszeitbudget in privaten Haushalten.' *Baden-Württemberg in Wort und Zahl*, Vol 23, pp173-178, 1975.